Go M·A·D!

Go Make A Difference

Edited and compiled by

ᴛʜᴇ Ecologist

www.theecologist.org

Sponsored by

042612

FRIENDS PROVI~~DENT~~ ~~THE BO~~DY SHOP

A Think Book

First published in 2001 by Think Publishing

Vigilant House,

120 Wilton Road,

London SW1V 1JZ

Tel: 020 7808 7535

Fax: 020 7808 7536

Email: watchdog@thinkpublishing.co.uk

First edition 2001

Researched and compiled by The Ecologist team

The Ecologist is the world's longest-running environmental magazine, covering
major issues such as globalisation, genetic modification, cancer and climate
change. It is published ten times a year, with over 68 pages packed with facts
and in-depth analysis.

Printed and bound by Cox and Wyman

Papers used by Think Publishing are natural, recyclable products made from
wood grown in sustainable forests. The manufacturing processes conform to the
environmental regulations of the country of origin.

ISBN 0-9541363-0-6

Thanks

We would like to thank Friends Provident and The Body Shop for their support, without which Go MAD! would not have been possible. A big thank you also must go to the Royal Society for the Protection of Birds (RSPB) for their encouragement and enthusiasm in the early days.

We also want to extend our thanks to Greenpeace and Friends of the Earth for their invaluable sources of information, as well as the other 200 organisations who helped compile this book.

Thanks also to Annabel Short for her perseverance in researching and compiling the tips, facts and contacts. And to Susannah McMicking for her editorial assistance.

Finally, to Edward Goldsmith, the founder of The Ecologist, whose values and tireless campaigning for the environment are the inspiration behind Go Make A Difference.

Go M·A·D!

Contents

Go M·A·D!

Intro

Zac Goldsmith

Editor, The Ecologist

Our finite world is being plundered, not by collective need but by greed, and the consequences, from climate change to species extinction, from chemical contamination to water depletion, are becoming ever clearer. The world has never had it so bad.

But the lifestyles we are accustomed to in the developed world are not inevitably destructive, and we do not need to adopt monk-like existences to save the world. We need, rather, to moderate and adapt.

Would fewer pesticides really be a sacrifice? Do we really need subsidised butter to be flown to our shops from New Zealand? Does the copious packaging that engulfs our modern products really improve those products? The answer is obviously 'no'. Our health and environment would be dramatically improved without these destructive and unpleasant additions.

So how do we make a difference? It's long been said that if you're not part of the solution, you're part of the problem. That can mean any number of things to any number of people, but certainly action is needed on every level. You cannot, after all, have clean lungs in a dirty city. It's hard for instance for many people to buy local food when local shops have been out-competed by politically-advantaged mega stores. It's hard to cycle to work when the transport infrastructure so favours cars. Without systemic, or policy change, our own actions are somewhat crippled, and we will continue to be part of the problem.

But we are also part of an economy that responds to consumer stimulation. When enough people power their homes with renewable energy, we will see a snowball effect, and before long, Britain will be carbon neutral. When enough people buy their food from local sources wherever possible, local economies will revive and our collective ecological footprint will dramatically shrink.

We can and must shout about the system, but we should do all we can to neutralise our own impacts at home. And while each individual action may appear to be inconsequential, collectively we can move mountains. It has been the efforts of teachers and mothers that have resulted in the removal of mobile phone masts from school buildings around the country. It was countless individual British shoppers who pressured the supermarkets into adopting a cautious approach to biotechnology, which consequently sent biotech shares into free-fall. And it was ordinary consumers in New Zealand whose concerns about the serious health implications of incineration led a third of all local authorities to adopt a zero waste strategy. The same campaign in Canberra, Australia has led to the routine recycling of 66% of all household and commercial waste, and a reduction by 42% in disposal to landfill sites. All this in just five years.

Go MAD! is primarily a guide to ecological living. It is full of fascinating facts, figures and suggestions for change in our own lives, each one of which if followed collectively, would make a tremendous difference. But it is also a guide to ecological renewal, with vital information on how we can all get involved in pushing for change at the policy and corporate level. Combined, this process is irresistible.

How to use this book

The 52 sections in Go MAD cover topics as diverse as cars, sleeping, love and pest control – which goes to show that every aspect of our lives has an impact on the environment. The aim of this book is to provide practical ways to make sure this impact is a positive rather than a negative one. In order to compile the tips we have contacted over 250 organisations – some are global-scale campaigning groups, others work in areas as specific as toy manufacture or promoting the use of cotton nappies. Whatever their size, they all play an invaluable role in helping people make a difference to the environment.

Likewise, small actions count just as much as big actions. We have organised the tips within each section in order of ascending "difficulty". The first tip in each section provides eye-opening background information on the topic. The second tip is either a tip for children (which doesn't mean that adults can't do it too!), or a tip which can easily become a part of your daily routine. As the tips in each section progress they gradually demand more effort. Tip seven is the "get out there, make your voice heard and find out more" tip. It points to places where you can find more information and gives details of specific campaigns you can get involved in.

How you can help

As well as getting out there and making a difference, please come back to us with your tips, too! There must be hundreds of brilliant ideas that we've missed – please let us know what they are.

You can send your tip by post or email and if we use it we'll send you a free copy of next year's edition of Go MAD. Please send your tip, along with any supporting information and contact details to:

Email: watchdog@thinkpublishing.co.uk
Post: Go MAD tips, The Ecologist, Unit 18,
             Chelsea Wharf, 15 Lots Road, London, SW10 0QJ.

Please remember to include your name, address and contact telephone number to ensure you receive a copy of next year's edition of Go MAD.

Birth

1

Cut down on baby paraphernalia

◆

When you are or your partner is pregnant one of the last things you may be thinking about is the environment. Parents-to-be and their families, encouraged by advertising, go on huge spending sprees with little consideration for the impact they are having on the environment, not to mention the money they are wasting on products they probably don't need or will only use for a short amount of time.

It's easy to spend £2,000 on baby paraphernalia before and during the first year of a child's life... but those first 21 months can be made calmer and easier by cutting down on extra products and making sure those you buy are simple, and natural.

Buy second-hand baby clothes

Why fork out on a swanky new romper suit your baby will grow out of in a few months? Second-hand baby clothes will be well-worn and therefore comfy. And if you aren't keeping them for future children of your own, pass them on again to friends or second-hand shops.

―――――――――― 3 ――――――――――

Use untreated cotton bedding

Synthetic bedding can expose a baby to formaldehyde, solvents and other chemicals, to which babies are particularly sensitive because their skin is much thinner than that of adults. All non-organic cotton is treated with pesticides and chemical fertilisers that stay in the cotton after it has been processed.

For organic cotton bedding and clothing try Gossypium www.gossypium.co.uk (01273 472211). You can also buy organic cotton clothing from Born. Their website has information on breast-feeding, alternative health and parenting www.first-born.co.uk (0117 924 5080).

―――――――――― 4 ――――――――――

Make a careful choice between breast and bottle

Breast feeding, according to certain baby organisations, reduces your baby's risk of illness and infections. Furthermore huge amounts of energy are used to produce formula milk from cow's milk, and artificial additives are added to the formulas. If you do need to buy formula milk, there are organic varieties available.

For breast feeding advice contact La Leche League www.laleche.org.uk (020 7242 1278) and for general feeding information, visit the National Childbirth Trust at www.nctpregnancyandbabycare.com or call the breastfeeding line on 0870 444 708.

5

Buy organic and GM-free food for your baby. Or make it yourself

Organic baby-food is already bought by 60% of mothers, and is available in most supermarkets and small retailers. Friends of the Earth have found high levels of pesticides in non-organic baby food. Pesticide residues have even more impact on babies than on adults as the amount they eat in proportion to their body weight is higher.

Visit Hipp at www.hipp.co.uk (0845 050 1351) and find out about Babynat at www.organico.co.uk (020 8340 0401). Both specialise in organic baby food.

6

Use natural soap for your baby

Soap has an excellent safety record – why expose your baby's skin unnecessarily to a cocktail of detergents, foam boosters, thickeners, preservatives, colourants and fragrances? Natural soaps are made from plant extracts and organic herbs instead of harsh petrochemicals. They use low-energy production methods and minimal packaging. Find out more from Simply Soaps at www.simplysoaps.com (07775 564 802).

7

Take Action with Babymilk Action

The World Health Organisation estimates that 1.5 million infants die worldwide each year because they are not breastfed, but instead given aggressively-marketed milk substitutes mixed with unsafe water. Where the water is unsafe a baby who is bottle fed is up to 25 times more likely to die as a result of diarrhoea than a baby who is breastfed. In 1981, an international marketing code was set up to regulate the industry, but companies continue to violate that code.

Baby Milk Action is part of the International Baby Food Action Network and campaigns to expose these violations and make milk substitute companies take responsibility for their actions. Find out how you can help at www.babymilkaction.org, or call 01223 464 420.

Cars

1

Don't drive the environment to destruction

Q. What's the link between your car and a hurricane?

A. Global warming.

90% of the world's cars are owned by people in the world's 16 wealthiest countries, which only account for a fifth of the world's population. But the effects of global warming caused by these cars are felt all across the world – people in developing countries such as the low-lying islands of the Pacific will be the most vulnerable to the flooding and extreme weather caused by climate change.

The world is now warming at the fastest rate for over 100,000 years. It's time for everyone to take responsibility. The UN's Intergovernmental Panel on Climate Change predicts that millions of people will die and millions of others will become environmental refugees as a result of global warming.

Cars are responsible for a fifth of the UK's emissions of CO_2 and the average car in the UK produces 4.5 tonnes of greenhouse gases a year. Not driving at all is obviously the best thing for the environment, but there are plenty of steps you can take to make driving less damaging.

2

KIDS – tell your parents to slow down!

Cars are more efficient at slower speeds. Driving at 50mph uses 25% less fuel than 70mph. Other ways you can improve your efficiency while driving are braking and accelerating gently, using high gears when the traffic allows it, and having your car serviced regularly.

3

Take public transport whenever possible

One litre of fuel will carry a person 4 miles in a large car, 5.5 miles in a small car, 31 miles in a bus with 40 passengers and 34 miles in a train with 300 passengers. A double-decker bus carries the same number of people as 20 full cars yet takes up one seventh of the road-space.

4

Recycle your car oil

Car oil contains toxic heavy metals such as lead, nickel and cadmium. One litre of car oil can contaminate one million litres of water, and oil poured directly onto the soil affects its fertility. Every year in the UK 13,000 tonnes of car oil are not collected for recovery, and so find their way into the sewers and watercourses.

Some recycling depots and petrol stations will recover your oil for you, and take it to have its particles filtered out. Contact the Oil Bank for more details on 0800 663 366.

Go M·A·D!

─── 5 ───
Join a car-sharing pool

There are thousands of cars with only one person in them clogging up the roads: car trips with just one person in the car account for 38% of journeys, and trips shared by two people 34%. Contact the Community Car Share Network: visit www.carclubs.org.uk, or call 01132 349 299.

─── 6 ───
Fit a fuel saver – cut emissions by 40%

By fitting a fuel-saving device into the fuel line that feeds your car engine you can reduce emissions of polluting gases by 40% and save at least 10% on your fuel costs. You can fit them onto any hydro-carbon fuelled vehicle (petrol, diesel, LPG) so even if you have an energy-efficient car you can still make it greener. Once installed you can forget about them, and they will last for one million miles of driving – yes, you can even transfer them from one vehicle to another if you need to. Visit www.powerplus.be, or call 01323 417 700.

─── 7 ───
Next time you buy a new car become a green driver

Choose a high efficiency model. Or buy an electric car, an LPG (propane and butane powered) or a hybrid car that runs on both petrol and electricity. Hybrid cars produce 75% less pollution than standard ultra-low-emission vehicles, and you can charge them at home. The Environmental Transport Association has a car buyers' guide with data on engine size, fuel consumption, noise and exhaust emissions for different models. Visit www.eta.co.uk, or call the ETA on 01932 828 882. Find out about LPG from the LP Gas Association at www.lpga.co.uk (01425 461612) and about electric cars from the Electric Car Association at www.electric-cars.org.uk (01823 480 196).

And remember to take part in next year's European Car Free Day. In 2001, 100 million people took part either by just not using their car, or participating in the street parties, park and ride schemes and alternative transport events that took place all over Europe. You've no excuse! Contact your local council or the Environmental Transport Association for details.

─Christmas─

Have a Green Christmas!

◆

A white Christmas is rare, so why not guarantee
yourself a Green one instead?

At Christmas we go into an all-consuming, all-disposing frenzy. Over the
Christmas period 2000, we spent a mammoth £12.5 billion on food,
drink and gifts. Our concerns for the environment get thrown out of the
window along with the wrapping paper, the dead Christmas tree and
the left-over roast potatoes... but it doesn't have to be that way.

There are simple steps you can take to be less wasteful without turning
into a Scrooge. Set yourself a challenge – how empty can you keep your
bins? One fifth more waste is created at Christmas than at other times
of the year. Create a system in the house to sort and store recyclable
goods before taking them to a recycling depot. When you are buying
goods, think about how much waste they will create: buying food and
drinks in large containers instead of several smaller ones will save you
pennies and help you keep your bin slim.

'I wonder
which is more
eco-friendly...
buying a plastic
Christmas tree
or cutting down
a real one.'

17

—— 2 ——

KIDS – make your own Christmas cards and decorations

An estimated 1.7 billion Christmas cards are sent each year in Britain, the equivalent of 200,000 trees, and hardly any of the cards sold on the high street are made from recycled paper. Old newspapers and magazines make great paper chains and scrap materials can be used to make Christmas tree decorations. This makes more sense than spending £20 on a sparkly angel which has been made by children in a far-eastern sweat-shop then flown half the way round the world to be thrown away after a few days perched on a Christmas tree.

—— 3 ——

Buy a UK-grown Christmas tree and take it to a recycling scheme

Five-and-a-half million Christmas trees are bought each year, most of which are thrown out after their use, creating enough tree waste to fill the Albert Hall three times over. Local Authorities run schemes which chip Christmas trees to make a park and garden mulch but in early 2001 only 750,000 trees were recycled. Phone your council to find out if it has a scheme. Better still, buy a tree with roots that you can plant in the garden and use for next year.

—— 4 ——

Use string, ribbon or scraps of wool for wrapping gifts instead of tape

Sticky-tape does not biodegrade and can only be used once, whereas string or wool can be used again and again. And so can the paper because it hasn't been messed up with sticky-tape marks – each year more than 8,000 tonnes of wrapping paper (50,000 trees-worth) is used on Christmas presents in the UK.

Only buy Fair Trade chocolate

We spend £700 million extra on chocolate at Christmas. In the last 10 years the price of cocoa beans has halved, but during the same period the price of a bar of chocolate in the UK has increased by two-thirds – so it's definitely not the farmers who are making the extra money. The Day Chocolate company, makers of 'Divine' chocolate, ensures their cocoa farmers are paid a fair price. In addition, the farmers are shareholders in the company. Visit www.divinechocolate.com, or call 020 7378 6550.

If you're buying a turkey, make it organic

Of the 10 million turkeys that we eat at Christmas in the UK most have been reared intensively in huge, windowless sheds holding up to 2,500 birds each. The birds have been genetically selected to grow as fast as possible, are fed antibiotics and are so overweight they cannot mate naturally. Appetising?

Give someone else a happy Christmas

Christmas can be the worst time of year for people who have no-one to share it with. Consider donating some money, or even your time, to a charity which works with the homeless, elderly people or those suffering from domestic violence. Think small! The mainstream charities which everyone knows about will be inundated with Christmas donations – choose a small, specific charity that really needs your help. And how about remaining loyal to it over the years with a direct debit?

For a register of all UK charities and their contact details go to www.charity-commission.gov.uk, or call 0870 333 0123. And you can be linked up to a local volunteering project by Timebank. Visit www.timebank.org.uk, or call 020 7401 5420.

Cleaning

1

There's nothing 'clean' about chemicals

When you're cleaning your house you're often doing the opposite to the environment, and also to your health. Our lifestyles have never been so full of chemicals – by the 1980s the world chemical output was 500 times greater than in 1940. There are now 60,000–70,000 synthetic chemicals in regular daily use.

One of the major sources of exposure to these chemicals is through cleaning products which we use every day in the home – so by simple changes of habit we can cut our exposure to them. Most companies (let alone advertisers!) don't specify the ingredients of their products, but usually they'll contain at least one of three harmful types of chemical. These are: 'bioaccumulative' chemicals that build up inside our bodies; 'persistent' chemicals that do not break down in the environment; and 'hormone-disrupting' chemicals that can interfere with our body's hormone systems.

The answer?
Don't use unnecessary chemicals and choose ecological alternatives.

Use low-phosphate washing-up liquid and washing powder

Phosphates are used as water-softeners, and when they are discharged into the water supply they stimulate excessive algal growth. These 'algal blooms' starve water of oxygen, killing plant and fish life, and they disrupt the sewage treatment process. For every litre of Persil you use, 20,000 litres of water are needed to treat it until it can re-enter our water system safely. Instead of phosphate-filled washing detergents use an EcoBall! They work by producing ionized oxygen that activates water molecules so they penetrate deep into clothing fibres, and use no harsh chemicals or detergents. They last for 1000 washes and cost only 3p a wash. Visit www.ecozone.co.uk, or call 0870 600 6969 for more details of this and other ecological washing products.

Avoid products containing chlorine

Chlorine is highly corrosive, capable of damaging the skin, eyes and other membranes. It irritates the lungs and research has linked exposure to chlorine with birth defects and cancer. Detergents transfer their chlorine into the air through a process called volatilisation – when you open the dishwasher the steamy mist that comes out is full of chlorine. Chlorine concentrations in the upper atmosphere have quadrupled over the past 25 years. Each chlorine atom released is capable of destroying tens of thousands of ozone molecules. Other chlorine-containing products to avoid are chlorine bleach, chlorinated disinfectant cleaners, mildew removers and toilet bowl cleaners. Find ecological alternatives at www.greenbrands.co.uk (0870 727 6868).

Use soap or ecological shampoo for cleaning rugs and upholstery

Many carpet and upholstery cleaners contain perchorethylene, a known carcinogen that can cause anaemia, damage to the liver, kidneys and nervous system. Others contain ammonium hydroxide, which is corrosive and irritates the eyes, skin and respiratory passages.

5

Use baking soda to clear your drains instead of abrasive powders

Many commercial drain cleaners contain corrosive and toxic products such as sodium or potassium hydroxide, hydrochloric acid and petroleum distillates that kill aquatic life and make water even more expensive to treat – there's no need for them! Flushing drains with a solution of boiling water, baking soda and vinegar then using a plunger will work just as well. And never flush cleaning products down the drain, they can corrode water pipes and kill sewage-eating bacteria.

6

Avoid commercial furniture polishes

Furniture polishes are petroleum distillates, which are flammable and have been linked with skin and lung cancer.
They also contain nitrobenzene, which is highly toxic and easily absorbed through the skin. Ecozone has alternatives, visit www.ecozone.co.uk, or call 0870 600 6969.

7

Become a toxic expert – learn about your brands!

Brands of cleaning products you have used for years may be highly toxic or polluting your home – their manufacturers will keep on making them as long as people buy them. So find out which brands are bad and why, and boycott them.

Greenpeace's campaign against toxins is a mine of information on how chemicals affect our lives. Their 'toxic kitchen' has details of the pros and cons of different products used in all parts of the home: visit www.greenpeace.org.uk/Products/Toxin, or call 01179 268 893.

Alternatively find out all about chemicals in cleaning products at www.arcania.co.uk/greentree/features/clean.htm.

Clothes

1

Dress to make a difference

Clothes – for most people anyway! – are an everyday part of life. So much so that rarely do we think about where they've come from. Who has made them? How far have they been transported? What exactly are they made of? What effect has their manufacture had on the environment?

Polyester and nylon, are made from non-renewable petro chemicals, their manufacture uses vast amounts of water and energy and they never biodegrade. And cotton is not as 'natural' as you may think: it is the world's most pesticide-sprayed crop. As well as buying second-hand clothes there are several places you can buy clothes made from natural and ecological materials.

Visit Ethical Consumer's Green Clothing Directory to find out where at www.ethicalconsumer.org, or call 0161 226 2929. Look out for the Oeko-Tex label that guarantees the manufacture of clothes has met strict environmental standards.

SWEAT
SHIRT
£25.00

SWEAT
SHOP
SHIRT
£4.99

---- 2 ----

KIDS – make a draft excluder – recycle and save energy at the same time!

Clothes don't just have to be worn – put old clothes to new uses. Once a jumper has been worn by all the members of the family and looks battered beyond use, its life is still not over. If not a draft excluder, how about using it for cleaning-rags, patchwork, or furniture stuffing?

---- 3 ----

Give old clothes to a recycling scheme

The fibre from all clothes can be shredded then re-woven to make new clothes – so there's no excuse for throwing them out. The Textile Recycling Association, Scope and Oxfam run schemes that do this. And your local charity shops will always be happy to be given last summer's fashions – someone out there will love them even if you don't. Make sure you close the loop too, by buying second-hand clothes.

Find out more about the TRA's Recyclatex Scheme on 01480 455249. Visit www.scope.org.uk, or call 0808 800 3333. Visit www.oxfam.org.uk, or call 01865 311 311.

---- 4 ----

Do you really need another T-shirt?

Picture your wardrobe - is it full-to-bursting with clothes that you've bought on a whim or in a rush, but never really worn? Save on energy and resources by really thinking about what you're buying, and spend just a little bit more on each item so you can wear it for years instead of months before it falls apart.

5

Avoid washing clothes at 50°C

No garment needs to be washed at 50°C. A clothing company can cut the energy used during the lifecycle of its clothes by 10% just by changing all its 50°C labels to 40°C. Marks and Spencer did this and saved the equivalent amount of energy needed to run all its 300 UK stores for four months. If you have clothes with 50°C on the label, write to the shop or manufacturer asking them to change all labels to 40°C.

6

Don't use commercial mothballs

Mothballs release napthalene vapour and dichlorobenzene (para-DCB) into the air. Para-DCB is a known human carcinogen, and repeated exposure to high levels can damage the nervous system and lungs. Napthalene does not cause cancer, but high levels can cause headache, fatigue, confusion, nausea and vomiting. Instead, make sure you store woollen items in air-tight boxes or use alternatives such as cedar chips or lavender flowers.

7

Think of the real fashion victims

The $20 million that Nike pay Michael Jordan to endorse its products for one year is equal to the total amount they pay Indonesian workers, each earning 20 cents an hour, to produce 19 million pairs of shoes, many of which were valued at as much as £100 a pair. But remember it's not only the major brands like Nike or the Gap who exploit cheap labour forces – they may get all the media attention, but other high street brands are just as guilty.

Consumer power does work to stamp out exploitation: following a boycott, BHS was the first UK company to stop sourcing from the repressive regime in Burma. Levis has a policy not to source from oppressive regimes, deciding not to operate in Haiti or El Salvador.

Write to retailers encouraging them to join the Ethical Trading Initiative (an umbrella group of companies aiming to improve workers' rights). Visit www.ethicaltrade.org, or call 020 7404 1463. And find out more about the good, bad and the ugly brands from the Clean Clothes Campaign at www.cleanclothes.org.

Community

1

Keep the local community alive within the global one

We have more ways to communicate than ever before. But while we can email people the other side of the world in seconds, we have often never had a conversation with our neighbours. We live in a world of communication, yet often forget how to communicate. Everybody complains that our communities are being destroyed, that local shops are disappearing and being replaced by chain restaurants, out of town supermarkets and mobile phone centres. But we all use them. They seem easier, more efficient, quicker. Do they really save you time though?

Rebuilding a sense of local community is one of the most rewarding ways that we can confront the rising tide of globalisation. Simply by being part of our local community, talking with the people who live around us, shopping in our local shops and contributing to the way that our area is run, we make a vital difference.

Go M·A·D!

KIDS – become one of the Woodcraft Folk

The Woodcraft Folk is a fast-growing organisation for people aged 6-20. It doesn't just involve woodcraft! It organises action-packed programmes based on environmental issues, and once a year an international camp that brings together woodcraft folk from all over the world. An original alternative to Scouts and Brownies! To find your nearest group, go to www.woodcraft.org.uk or call 020 8672 6031.

—————— *3* ——————

Take old magazines to your local doctor's surgery

Whether it's Cosmopolitan or The Economist, someone out there would like to read it. Doctors' surgeries don't have the budgets to spend on lots of magazines, and while sitting waiting for the doctor we all could do with something to keep us occupied.

—————— *4* ——————

Participate!

There are hundreds of ways of getting involved in your local community. They can be simple, no-effort actions such as talking to people in your local shops, or time-saving initiatives such as setting up a baby-sitting circle. If you do have more time, how about applying to become a governor in a local school, or a Justice of the Peace?

5

LETS work locally to make a difference

LETS (Local Exchange Trading System) members exchange and share goods and services with one another, using a special currency of LETS units instead of money. The services exchanged include dog-walking, house-sitting, massage, aromatherapy and legal services. There are currently over 480 LETS schemes in the UK, empowering individuals and building on ties within the community. Visit www.letslinkuk.org, or call 020 7607 7852.

6

Set up a community recycling scheme

Not all local councils provide efficient recycling projects – if yours doesn't, set up your own! You may be entitled to recycling credits: many local authorities give money to community groups who collect materials for recycling, based on the savings made by recycling the household waste they collect. Wastewatch has details of how to go about it: visit www.wastewatch.org.uk or call 0870 243 0136.

7

Aim to sustain!

Help your local area move towards sustainability by getting involved with Common Ground www.commonground.org, that revitilises local sustainable traditions, or BioRegional www.bioregional.com (020 8773 2322). Bioregional works on the green ideal of local production for local needs. Its projects range from Local Lavender, which is reviving south London's lavender industry on areas of wasteland, to building energy-efficient housing, to locally grown food.

Find out about your council's Local Agenda 21 strategies, too. Local Agenda 21 was set up at the 1992 Earth Summit in Rio and aims to help communities achieve sustainability through co-operation. You can find out if your council is involved from the Improvement and Development Agency (IDEA). Visit www.la21-uk.org.uk, or call 020 7296 6599.

Compost

1

Give nutrients back to the soil

◆

Almost a third of our domestic waste could go straight onto the compost heap. Instead, 27 million tonnes of organic waste such as food scraps and tea bags go to landfill each year. The crazy thing is, once there it is deprived of oxygen and does not biodegrade. There is no reason why it should not be turned into compost, returning the nutrients and energy from your leftover food back to the soil where they can be reused.

Composting is a direct way of understanding what we need to do to change the world - that is, respect its cyclic patterns instead of using it as a coneyor-belt leading directly from resource to waste. If you make your own compost you are recycling your waste, and reaping the benefits visibly as you watch your garden grow.

Bert introduces some fibre to his compost bin.

KIDS – go MAD with worms

Set up a worm-composting bin, either inside your house or out.
Worms eat your kitchen waste and convert it into rich dark compost
by passing it through their bodies. Each worm can recycle half its own
bodyweight of waste every day – if you have a bin-full of worms, that's
a lot of composting. You can buy worm-composting bins, but why not
make your own? The best type of worms to use are tiger worms and
red worms. Contact Wiggly Wigglers for more details. Visit
www.wigglywigglers.co.uk, or call 0800 216 990.

3

Start a compost heap

Compost bins are easy to get hold of at garden centres, but even
better, make your own from old tyres, scrap timber, bricks or wire
mesh. By building your own bin you can recycle materials which might
otherwise find their way to the scrap heap.

Compost is soil's gold. As well as recycling all your leftover scraps of
uncooked food, the end result will be a rich soil treatment that will
help your garden flourish. Visit The Henry Doubleday Research
Association at www.hdra.org.uk/gh_comp.htm (02476 303 517) and
Waste Watch at www.wastewatch.org.uk (0870 243 0136). Both have
helpful information on how to make your own compost.

4

Feed your compost heap with fibre

All your paper and card which cannot be recycled can be composted.
That includes tissues, kitchen towels, the tubes from toilet rolls, cereal
boxes and egg boxes. Like people, compost heaps need fibre to keep
healthy (otherwise they go soggy!). Fibre keeps air spaces in the
compost, so your heap will be bursting with beneficial creepy-crawlies.

Give your flower beds some coffee

Did you know that coffee-grounds are perfect compost material? Next time you're about to tip out the coffee pot, tip it onto the flowerbeds instead of into the bin. Or onto your compost heap! Other good things to compost are old prunings, straw and hay, hamster and rabbit bedding, eggshells and autumn leaves. Avoid cooked food and meat.

— 6 —

No garden? No excuse

Find out where your nearest community composting project is. And if there isn't one in your area, set one up. The Community Composting Network provides composting sites around the UK that each serve about 100 households. The compost made from their organic waste is distributed around the community either for free or at a cheap price, and it's also used in local parks. Contact the Community Composting Network at www.othas.org.uk, or call 0114 258 0483.

— 7 —

Save our peat bogs!

Lowland raised peat bogs are one of the rarest and most ancient wildlife habitats in the UK, and a haven for unique flora and fauna. But their rich valuable peat is also a prime target for gardeners. Gardening is one of our fastest growing pastimes. It now accounts for 70% of all the peat used in the UK, with gardeners increasing their use of peat by 50% between 1993 and 1997. The area of lowland raised bog in the UK has diminished by an astonishing 94%, from an original 95,000 hectares to approximately 6,000 hectares today. So either make your own, or buy peat-free composts that are available in most garden centres and DIY stores.

Find out more about our disappearing peat bogs and what you can do to help at www.plantlife.org.uk/html/campaigns_peat.htm. Plant Life (020 7808 0100) works for the conservation of wild plants in Britain. It is a mine of information on British plants and why it's important to protect them. The Scottish Wildlife Trust also has a peat bog campaign at www.swt.org.uk/peatland/peatland.html.

 Go M·A·D!

Cooking

1

Bring life back into the kitchen

◆

Life used to revolve around the kitchen. Now it's often a question of rush in, pop a pre-prepared meal into the microwave, wolf it down and then hurry off to the rest of the day's activities.

Taking the time out to cook not only creates a peaceful and relaxing interlude in the day, which you can share with other people, but it means you can eat better too. It enables you to select ingredients which are locally produced and which you know haven't been processed beyond recognition.

'Wait a second...
Is that organic?'

KIDS – get cooking!

Next time you go to a birthday party, how about taking some biscuits you've made? If you just learn how to cook one dish a month, in a year's time you'll have twelve different dishes you can prepare for your friends and family.

—————— 3 ——————

Don't overcook vegetables – switch off the heat when they are nearly cooked

Vegetables lose flavour and vitamins when they are overcooked, and by turning off the heat earlier you will save energy (the water will continue boiling for a while due to the residual heat).

—————— 4 ——————

Save energy with your saucepans!

There are several ways in which heat, and therefore energy, is wasted when you use a saucepan to cook. Use the right size pan, and only use the water you need to cover the food you are boiling. Make sure the pan base just covers the ring of an electric cooker and if you are using a gas hob adjust the flame to suit the size of the pan – if the flames come round the side, you are heating the kitchen too!

And when you wash your pans, save water by leaving them to soak rather than washing them in running water.

5

Use baking soda and water instead of commercial oven cleaners

Oven cleaners contain potassium, sodium hydroxide and ammonia, which are corrosive and toxic – do you really want to expose your food to them? There's no need to spend money on dangerous chemicals when baking soda does the job just as well.

6

Invest in a slow cooker

You don't have to use an oven or a hob to cook. A slow cooker uses little more electricity than a light bulb, and because the food is cooked gently it loses less of its vitamins and flavour than in other cooking methods. Steamers and pressure cookers are also excellent and economical ways of preserving the taste and goodness of food when you cook it.

7

Take your time!

Where else but Italy would a movement called 'SlowFood' have emerged? The ethos behind SlowFood is to bring the pleasure back to eating by taking your time. That includes the time involved in growing the food, preparing it, and cooking it, giving the control over what we eat back to the consumer. And with slowness, comes diversity.

Due to the mass production of our food we in fact end up with less and less choice. In 1900, for example, there were about 200 species of artichokes in Italy but now there are only a dozen. The SlowFood movement is a reaction against this, a reaction that is (quickly!) growing in momentum, with over 60,000 members in 35 different countries. Join up at www.slowfood.com, where you can also be updated on slow food initiatives all round the world and visit the SlowFood Planet, which has information about the best slow eateries around the globe.

─Cosmetics─

─ 1 ─

Be a natural beauty

◆

Women (and men!) can absorb up to two kilogrammes of chemicals through toiletries and cosmetics each year. And 2,000 cosmetic ingredients found in products which we take for granted, such as skin creams, shampoos and perfumes, can be harmful to our health.

The standards which apply to food, in which the manufacturers must tell the truth when they say 'free from artificial colourings, preservatives and flavourings' don't apply to cosmetics.

So a product that claims to be 'natural' may be far from it: the ingredients may have been natural at the outset, but by the time they reach your skin they have been artificially processed. In fact, for a commercial product to call itself 'natural' it only has to consist of 1% of that natural product. Anita Roddick of the Body Shop has said that the marketing blurb on cosmetic labels often amounts to 'a scandalous lie.' Are you buying it?

2

Drink 2.5 litres of water a day

Our blood is 92% water, so if you're not drinking enough your complexion will look tired and dry: drink water and you'll be able to let your face speak for itself without foundation. Avoid anti-wrinkle creams – they contain products such as alpha and beta hydroxy acids (AHAs and BHAs), known as 'skin-peelers', which dissolve the outer layer of your dead skin cells, to which the skin reacts by growing back an even thicker, tougher layer!

3

Use natural fragrances

Your extravagant bottle of perfume could contain a mixture of 600 synthetic chemicals. Over 5,000 chemicals are used in fragrance manufacture, 95% of which are made from petroleum and many of which are designated as hazardous. As an alternative, use natural perfumes and aromatherapy oils which can be used on the skin. Find out more from Culpeper at www.culpeper.co.uk or 01223 891 196. A directory of aromatherapy suppliers and practicioners is available at www.fragrant.demon.co.uk/ukaromas.html.

4

If you buy a cosmetic product in a plastic tub *and* a box, leave the box at the check-out

Can you think of anything more wasteful than double-packaging? Instead, buy refillable bottles. The Body Shop has set up a pioneering refill scheme and even gives discounts when you re-use your bottles! Visit www.the-body-shop.com, or call 01903 731 500. Write to your favourite cosmetics company, asking them to set up a refill scheme.

Go M·A·D!

Only buy nail polish free from DBP

DBP(dibutyl phthalate), used to make nail polish flexible, has been linked to reproductive problems. Tests have found DBP in 37 popular brands of nail polish – and levels of DBP are five times higher in young women than in other people.

If a fragrance says 'musk' on the bottle, don't touch it!

Artificial musks are 'bioaccumulative': they build up in body fat, blood and breast milk, and in the environment. Other side affects can be headaches, dizziness, rashes and respiratory problems. Some are also hormone disrupters, interfering with the hormones which regulate our daily bodily functions. They are found mainly in perfumes and cosmetics, but also in laundry detergents – to find out more, visit www.foe.co.uk, or call 020 7490 1555.

Boycott animal-tested beauty products

A label that says 'not tested on animals' is not always telling the whole truth. Just because the finished product has not been tested on animals, it doesn't mean that the individual ingredients have not been tested on animals. Look out for the Humane Cosmetics Standard 'rabbit and stars' logo. It is an internationally recognised guarantee that the product has not been tested on animals at any stage. A full list of HCS approved products is available free from the British Union for the Abolition of Vivisection.

Visit www.buav.org, or call 020 7700 4888. You can sign a petition at this site to persuade the European Parliament to pass legislation banning the sale of cosmetics tested on animals and the testing itself in all EU countries. Beauty without Cruelty can also send you a list of companies which produce cosmetics without cruelty to animals. Write to Beauty without Cruelty, 74 Oldfield Rd, Hampton, TW12 2HR, or call 020 8979 8156

Cycling

--- 1 ---

Get out of your car and on your bike

Sick of traffic jams? If all the cars in Britain were lined up head to tail they would stretch twice round the world, and car traffic is expected to increase by 22% by 2010. Unless, that is, everyone gets on their bikes. There are more bikes than cars in the UK, but most of them sit at home unused - partly because road congestion puts people off using them!

Have you ever driven to the gym to spend forty minutes on a cycling machine? A 10% increase in the number of people riding a bike regularly would lead to a 4% reduction of people with heart disease, saving hundreds of millions a year in healthcare. And it would give the environment, and people, some breathing space.

KIDS – go on a family bike ride

A recent BUPA study found that obesity figures among children have doubled in the last decade. 33% of boys and 38% of girls aged two to seven don't get the recommended amount of exercise. The most worrying figures are among adolescents: 64% of 15-year-old girls are classed as being 'inactive'. For active, outdoor holiday inspiration, contact Bicycle Beano at www.bicycle-beano.co.uk, or call 01982 560 471.

—— 3 ——

Use your bike for all journeys under two miles

Catalytic converters that cut down on a car's carbon monoxide emissions only start working after you have driven for two miles. Yet 25% of car trips in the UK are less than two miles and 58% are less than five miles.

Road transport now constitutes over 70% of all carbon monoxide emissions in the UK.

—— 4 ——

Give your old bike a new lease of life – recycle it

Bike recycling projects make bikes which seem destined for scrap look as good as new. They are often community activities that provide jobs for people who've had a hard time finding work. Find your nearest project at www.wastepoint.org/wasteconnect. Or cut someone's trek to collect water, reach fields or towns in a developing country by up to three hours a day by donating your bike to ReCycle. Visit www.re-cycle.org, or call 01206 382 207.

5
Get an electric bike

Imagine a form of transport that costs 1.5p a mile to run, gives off no emissions and is quiet as a mouse. Electric bikes are the cleanest motorised vehicles on the roads. If you bear in mind that a car travelling in a city centre during 'rush' (!) hour spends 28% of its time stationary – and the same usually goes for public transport – an electric bike is the best way to get to work, gliding past queues at 15 miles an hour. Visit www.powabyke.com, or call 01225 446 878.

6
Reclaim the streets!

Cyclists, runners, walkers, in fact anyone who doesn't drive a car, are being squeezed off our streets.
Critical Mass bike rides are a peaceful, effective form of protest using bike-power to spread the message that it's time the streets were given back to the people. Find out about rides near you, or if you're feeling adventurous, abroad, at www.critical-mass.org.

7
Campaign to make it easier for everyone to use their bike

The National Cycle Network (NCN) will provide a 10,000-mile bike route around the UK by 2005. It will get people on their bikes, protect green sites from development and create wildlife corridors. It will also have links to schools, railway stations, offices and shopping centres. Visit www.sustrans.org.uk, or call 01179 268893.

And don't miss the largest cycling extravaganza in the world: since 1923 the Cyclists' Touring Club has organised the Festival of Cycling (it used to be called National Bike Week). All over the country individuals, schools, businesses and community groups take part in the festival to show how enjoyable cycling can be. Why don't you? Get all the info from the Cyclists' Touring Club. Visit their website at www.ctc.org.uk, or call 01483 417 217.

Death

1

Make a difference in death as well as life

When we die, everything stops. Or does it? In ecology, death is seen as part of the cycle of life, necessary for the continuation of other lives. While we may not be around to appreciate it ourselves, we can make a difference to the environment in death as well as life. The green funeral movement is one of the fastest-growing environmental movements in the UK.

In 1993, there was only one Green or woodland burial site in the UK – now there are over 130, run by local authorities, farmers and wildlife trusts. A Green funeral can also be more personal than a conventional one, with poems, songs and readings chosen by the deceased person, or their friends and family. And as more and more people choose to be buried in natural surroundings, in biodegradable coffins or shrouds, they are helping to protect our woodlands and wild places.

41

KIDS – pick your own flowers to take to a funeral

The wire and cellophane that comes with bought flower arrangements not only uses up resources but also becomes an eyesore around the grave once the flowers have died, taking years to decompose.

Even better than picked flowers that will soon die, why not take a rooted plant which can be planted by the grave?

—————— *3* ——————

Go for burial instead of cremation

In the UK, 74% of people are cremated – the largest proportion in Europe. Cremation releases toxins into the atmosphere such as hydrogen chloride and formaldehyde, and 11% of mercury emissions come from crematoria.

—————— *4* ——————

How about a cardboard coffin – or even making your own?

Each year, 437,000 wooden coffins are burned in the UK. Is it really worth sacrificing all those trees for our dead bodies? Cardboard coffins are biodegradable and much cheaper than wooden coffins, costing as little as £50. For a truly personal coffin you could even make your own! The Natural Death Centre has details, visit www.naturaldeath.co.uk, or call 020 8208 2853.

Go M·A·D!

Have a tree planted in your memory or go MAD and be buried in a wood

No hippy fad, there are now over 130 woodland burial sites in the UK. Being buried in a wood returns your body to nature, carbon is locked underground and land is saved from development. Many woodland burial sites are run by farmers and wildlife trusts. And what better headstone could you have than a living tree? Visit www.naturaldeath.org.uk, or call 020 8208 2853. Or try the Funeral Company at www.thefuneralcompanyltd.com (01908 225 222).

— 6 —

Taking your organs with you? Donate them instead!

Over 5,000 people are currently waiting for a transplant. Many of them will die because they won't receive an organ in time. Pick up a donor card from your local doctor's surgery, get one online at www.nhsorgandonor.net, or phone 0845 60 60 400.

— 7 —

Keep campaigning after you've gone – write an eco-will

In 1999, £1.2billion was given to charities in 86,000 legacies – four times the amount given by the corporate sector. Why don't you write an ethical will? Visit www.ethicalwill.com and preserve your legacy of values and hopes for future generations. Leave something for a charity or environmental organisation which means a lot to you. And on the subject of wills, if relatives are not going to need your old furniture, how about leaving it to a local community centre, school or old people's home?

Go M·A·D!

DIY and Decorating

1

What are you really doing when you do it yourself?

The back-to-back home improvement programmes that appear on TV and the radio may inspire you to give your house a flashy makeover. But often the products and methods they promote are designed to look good, without considering the harm they can do to your health and the environment. In terms of energy and toxicity, buildings and construction are among the most wasteful and polluting areas of modern life. But there are ecological alternatives.

The Association of Environment Conscious Building (www.aecb.net, tel: 01559 370 908) and the Green Building Store (www.greenbuildingstore.co.uk, tel: 01484 854 898) will help you choose which products to buy and which to avoid. In the end though, if you really want to be happy with the place you live, it's a state of mind, not a coat of paint that will make the difference. And as you anguish over which shade of buttermilk to paint the hall, remember those without homes – buy the Big Issue.

2

Donate your leftover paint

Of the 300 million litres of paint sold in the UK each year, 6.2 million litres remain unused. The Community Re-Paint scheme run by Save Waste and Prosper runs paint collection schemes. It sorts the paint and redistributes it to local community projects and housing services. Find out more at www.communityrepaint.org.uk.

3

Check the labels and avoid solvent-based paints

Modern gloss paints can contain up to 50% solvents and VOCs (volatile organic compounds) which enter the surrounding air throughout the paint's lifetime – inhalation and absorption through the skin of VOCs affect the nervous system, irritate the eyes, nose and throat and damage internal organs. The World Health Organisation says that decorators are faced with a 40% increased chance of lung cancer. The high product-to-waste ratio for solvent paints means that 30 tonnes of waste are produced for every tonne of product made. Instead, use natural paints made from plant and mineral bases. There are several companies that make or sell them. Visit www.ecosolutions.co.uk, or call 01934 844 484; www.ecospaints.com, or call 01539 732 866; or www.greenshop.co.uk, tel: 01452 770 629.

4

Avoid chipboard and MDF

Chipboard and MDF (medium density fibreboard) have a high formaldehyde content, a recognised carcinogen which also irritates the lungs, throat and eyes. It can take two to three years before a product has finished releasing formaldehyde fumes. Instead, use softwood or European plywood, and for kitchen worktops use conifer. Make sure that any wood you use is from a sustainable source – either from a managed Scandinavian source or, even better, with the Forest Stewardship Council symbol on it.

FSC

Rent power tools or share with neighbours

That small, cheap electric drill was probably made in a sweatshop on the other side of the world, its production and transportation consuming unnecessary amounts of energy and causing pollution. Why not hire tools, or invest in more durable ones that can be pooled with neighbours? Letslink will help: www.letslinkuk.org (020 7607 7852)

Avoid standard insulation materials (mineral fibre insulation or sheet insulation)

Mineral fibre insulation can increase the risk of skin and lung cancers; sheet insulation made from polystyrene or polyurethane is manufactured using gases that deplete the ozone layer; and loose-fill insulation such as Vermiculite is made from naturally-occurring minerals processed at high temperatures, using vast amounts of energy. There are many alternatives available made from materials such as sheep's wool, newspaper, cork, cellulose or foamed glass. Visit www.greenbuildingstore.co.uk, or call 01484 854 898.

Campaign for the re-use of empty homes

For every homeless person in England there are seven empty homes. There are 100,000 empty homes in London alone, and almost 800,000 throughout the UK. Unused housing puts unnecessary pressure for development on green field sites, wastes resources, and creates ghost areas and crime hotspots in towns and cities. The Empty Houses Agency campaigns to bring as many of these houses as possible back into use. Take part in their 'The Ball's in Your Court' campaign, which is lobbying the government to allow local authorities to implement 100% council tax on long-term empty houses. Or join in the Community Action on Empty Houses campaign – find out about campaigns in your local area against the loss of greenfield space, urban decay or homelessness. Find out how you can help at www.emptyhomes.com or by calling 020 7828 6288.

Drink

Drink to a healthy environment

While water used to be the only drink available, and still is in most parts of the world, many of us are now substituting it with fizz, with flavour, with colourings in fancy packaging. They may keep our taste buds happy, but not our bodies, the environment, or local economies. Two companies control 77% of the soft drinks market: Coca-Cola and PepsiCo. They have swept their way through the developing world, flooding the market of locally-produced drinks and replacing healthier drinks in children's diets. Coke's active ingredient is phosphoric acid, which can dissolve a T-bone steak in two days, or a nail in four.

Back in 1969, 54% of babies who were hospitalised for malnourishment in Ndolo in Zambia had the diagnosis 'Fantababy' written at the foot of their beds. Their parents had fed them Coke and Fanta believing it to be the best drink for their children – a problem reflected all across the developing world. The Chairman of Coca-Cola is on record as saying 'The only business we don't want, is the business that does not exist.' Do you want to drink to his health?

'What's your poison, mate?'

2

Make your own drinks

Squeeze your own fruit juices, invent flavours never seen before. Make your own lemonade. You'll find that you can use locally grown, organic fruits and make a drink that is cheaper than any you can buy, healthier, and much, much tastier.

3

Rip up the plastic rings from packs of beer

Plastic rings are invisible in the water, so pose a real danger to aquatic life. Seals get their heads trapped in the rings, and they either choke or starve to death. Small seabirds get their wings trapped, and larger ones catch the rings around their bills when they dive for food.

4

Always buy Fair Trade tea and coffee

In 1998, farmers received 14% of the retail price of a jar of instant coffee – in 2001 that figure was just 7%. They rely on moneylenders who set the prices for coffee, and then charge the farmers exorbitant interest. If everyone in the UK bought one jar of Fair Trade coffee a month, 2.5 million people (the farmers and their families) would benefit. Buying fairly traded goods also means farmers resist the temptation of growing cocoa, the raw material for cocaine, instead. Visit www.fairtrade.org, or call 020 7405 5942.

Choose wine with natural corks

The increased use of plastic corks is threatening the unique habitat of the oak cork woodlands in Spain and Portugal. These woodlands not only produce over 80% of the world's cork, but they also provide a valuable habitat for livestock and wildlife. 42 species of bird depend on them, including the Spanish imperial eagle, which has a global population of only 130 pairs. Intensive agriculture is already encroaching on this area, and the growth of the plastic cork industry is further increasing the problem. Also the manufacture and recycling of plastic corks is energy-consuming and polluting.

6

Drink tap or filtered water instead of buying bottled

Despite the claims on its enticing packaging, bottled water is no better for you than tap water – in some cases it *is* tap water – and is sold at up to 1,000 times the price. Tap water is stringently tested for contaminants but bottled water may contain traces of the plastics the bottle is made from. There's also the energy waste in bottling, packaging and transportation: according to the WWF, every year 1.5 million tonnes of plastic are used to bottle water. A quarter of the 89 billion litres of water bottled worldwide annually are consumed outside their country of origin.

7

Support local breweries and pubs

The ingredients in a local beer might travel a total of 600 miles, but a beer from a major brewer can accumulate as many as 24,000 miles of transport. Currently four brewers dominate 83% of the market in the UK. Small breweries suffer from having to pay the same level of duty on alcohol as the large ones. In Germany, a Progressive Beer Duty system to help smaller breweries has been in operation for many years. In the UK, The Society of Independent Brewers is trying to impose a similar duty. For more information see www.siba.co.uk or write to the Siba Office, 16 Eversley Road, London SE7 7LD.

See also www.camra.org.uk, or call the Campaign for Real Ale on 01727 867 201. CAMRA campaigns tirelessly on behalf of beer manufacturers and drinkers.

Eating Out

1

Go MAD in restaurants!

◆

Consumerism has led us to expect fast, efficient service and a vast range of exotic ingredients and dishes. But all this comes at a price which is paid not only by you but also by the environment. The energy, resources and waste involved in the 'eating-out' industry are growing exponentially. It's worth remembering that if everyone in the world consumed at the rate of the highest consumers in the West, we would need five worlds to support us all. But it is possible to choose places to eat which have the minimum impact on the environment...

'For *what we are about to receive may the Lord let it not contain any Mad Cow disease, pesticides, E-coli bacteria, nitrates...*'

Choose organic options on the menu

There are more and more organic restaurants appearing on the scene – you can find their details from the Organic Directory at www.soilassociation.org/SA/Directory.nsf. But other restaurants and cafés often have organic choices available on the menu, which entail less pesticide use, and less energy consumption in their production.

3

Break the chain – eat at an independent local restaurant this weekend

Spread the profit! As chains of cafés and bars take over the high streets, small independent restaurants are struggling to compete. If we want our communities to have a flavour of their own, rather than just replicate the same brand names up and down every street, we have to give them the income to survive.

4

Avoid eating tuna – especially bluefin

There has been a seven-fold increase in tuna catches in the South Pacific since 1972, and as the price for tuna is so high, illegal fishing fleets are also going out to make a catch. In 2000, one fish sold for £55,000 wholesale at a Japanese market! The booming demand for tuna – especially raw tuna in sushi bars – is endangering the species. The bluefin is among the top five on the WWF Endangered Seas Campaign's list of fish species needing immediate action to avoid extinction. Bluefin, or 'toro'-is a favourite on sushi menus.

Ask the café or restaurant if it recycles its glass

Britain's 57,000 pubs and 70,000 restaurants and hotels use about 350,000 tonnes of glass a year. At the moment 80% of this goes to landfill, even though all of it could be recycled. If a restaurant's reason for not recycling is that local collection schemes are inadequate, suggest they team up with other restaurants to lobby the council to get a scheme going. Ring the Recycling Helpline on 01686 640600 to find out what schemes are currently available.

Support restaurants with small menus!

Generally, the larger the menu (unless each item is a variety on an identical theme), the more different types of food the restaurant has to have ready for consumption every day, and the more food will go to waste.

Boycott McDonald's

Need we say more? And for McDonald's, read also Kentucky Fried Chicken, Burger King and other fast food chains. McDonald's spends more than $2 billion a year broadcasting its glossy image to the rest of the world, but to hear the other, not so flattering side of the coin go to www.mcspotlight.org. The site will also tell you how you can campaign to help wrest the world from McDonald's all-consuming influence on the environment, its employees, its customers and other businesses. McSpotlight organises an International Boycott McDonald's Day and its 'Beyond McDonald's' section has detailed information on the tentacle-effect of other major corporations.

Go M·A·D!

Education

1

Make green beginnings

◆

Habits die hard – if you're brought up thinking Green, it's easier to stay thinking Green. Schools are the perfect place for environmental initiatives. They are crowded and busy places that consume a lot of resources. Environmental projects can help create a sense of community and participation while providing excellent teaching resources. And who knows, children may start bringing their good habits into the home and influencing their parents!

Meanwhile, we need to put the brakes on the increasing corporate takeover of our schools. In a school in America, for example, PepsiCo donated $2 million to build a school football stadium in exchange for exclusive rights to sell its soft drinks in all of the 140 district schools and to advertise in school gymnasiums and on athletics fields. That deal is estimated to earn the company $7.3 million over seven years. Education or exploitation?

'In this one I can hear the sound of traffic!'

2

Travel to school on foot or by public transport

At 8.50am, one in five cars on urban roads is taking children to school. One quarter of children travel to school by car, twice as many as 20 years ago. Contrary to popular belief, in slow-moving traffic pollution levels are actually higher inside the car than out. Children who walk to school are usually fitter than those who are dropped at the gate, and arrive for lessons more alert. Get involved in Sustran's Safe Routes to Schools initiative that is campaigning to get more children travelling to school on foot www.sustrans.org.uk or call 01179 268 893.

3

Get planting

Growing food is a fun way of learning the life cycle of a plant and becoming aware of where food comes from other than supermarket packets! And you don't need a garden. Herbs can be grown on windowsills, and carrots, tomatoes and potatoes can be grown in buckets on a balcony. At school, you can create a conservation area where you can work together with your classmates to make your own living, growing garden.

4

Put recycling bins in the classrooms

Think how much paper gets thrown away in schools each day, all of which could be recycled. Get a recycling scheme going at school and, if you're feeling keen, join the Schools Waste Action Club (SWAC) that combines recycling with lessons on waste, and a waste-reduction points system. Waste Watch has details www.wastewatch.org.uk. Follow links to 'projects' then 'education', or call 0870 243 0136.

Bring the countryside into the classroom

The countryside is a fantastic learning resource and studies have found that children who spend time learning outdoors and in close contact with nature often develop better interaction and initiative skills. Children living in urban areas often miss out on its benefits. The Countryside Foundation is an education charity that provides exciting learning materials to bring the countryside closer to home. Its website also has an activities section for young visitors. Visit www.countrysidefoundation.org.uk or call 01422 885 566 for more information. How about going on nature rambles too? Find out where your nearest 'wild places' are on the Friends of the Earth website www.foe.co.uk/wildplaces.

Make your school an energy-saver

UK schools account for 25% of public sector energy costs, spending around £350 million on energy and releasing 8 million tonnes of CO_2 each year. But there are several quick and easy ways to cut down on school energy consumption, such as installing energy-efficient lightbulbs. Find out what your school can do at www.schoolenergy.org.uk or call 01942 332 273.

Don't let education become a commodity, say NO to GATS

Students, teachers, campuses… normally we don't think of these as profit-making resources, or the institution of education as a market. But with the General Agreement on Trade in Services (GATS), all this may be up for grabs. GATS could start to replace the principles of learning with those of profit-making. Find out more at www.corpwatch.org/trac/feature/education. For indepth analysis, essays and comment go to www.xs4all.nl/~ceo/gatswatch/p_critique.html. Other organisations fighting against GATS are Education International at www.ei-ie.org, the Council of Canadians at www.canadians.org and the students' campaigning group, People and Planet. Vist their website at www.peopleandplanet.org or call 01865 245678.

Energy

— 1 —

Take responsibility for global warming

Each one of us is responsible for global warming. Quite simply, it is the greatest environmental threat facing the world and it is happening at a faster rate than ever predicted. The amount of oil used over the next ten years will exceed all the oil consumed in the first five decades of the last century. The scale of consumption is so vast that major changes need to come from governments and industry. But we too can play our part. One quarter of the UK's overall CO_2 emissions come from our homes. An average house produces 6 tonnes of carbon dioxide every year, more than the average car – so non-car drivers are not exempt from responsibility!

Find out more about energy saving from the Energy Savings Trust at www.saveenergy.co.uk (0845 727 7200) or from Energy Efficiency at www.energy-efficiency.gov.uk (0800 585 794).

Go M·A·D!

When you make a cup of tea or coffee boil only the amount of water you need

If everybody did this for just one day we could save enough energy to light every street lamp in the UK for the following night.

— 3 —

Turn appliances off instead of switching to standby

A VCR on standby uses almost as much current as one playing a tape. When the standby light is on, so is the appliance, so it's still using energy! Every year, VCRs in the UK use £113 million, and TVs £50 million worth of electricity just waiting to be switched on. If everyone switched their TV right off at night the UK could save enough energy to power a town the size of Basingstoke.

— 4 —

Turn the iron off when you have only one thing left to iron

It will still be hot enough to iron well, and although it may seem like a tiny action, gets us into the habit of making small, energy-saving changes that will collectively make a big difference to our world.

57

Share appliances with your neighbours

How often do you actually use that steam carpet cleaner? As well as saving on energy this is a way of forming links within the local community. LETS schemes are a good way of organising tool-pools: find out more at www.letslinkuk.org, or call 020 7607 7852.

—————————— *6* ——————————

Go MAD with alternative sources of energy

There are all sorts of small-scale renewable systems that you can use in your home which don't cost the earth. They include solar water heaters, solar panels and wind generators. For information about domestic wind turbines, contact The British Wind Energy Association at www.bwea.com (020 7402 7102). Two excellent sources of information on renewables in general are the Centre for Alternative Energy at www.cat.org.uk (01654 702 400) and the National Energy Foundation renewables at www.greenenergy.org.uk (01908 665555).

—————————— *7* ——————————

Force electricity suppliers to clean up their act – buy Green electricity

You can now choose between electricity suppliers, and some are far Greener than others – not always for a higher price. Get hold of the free leaflet 'Guide to Buying Green Energy' from Friends of the Earth. Visit www.foe.co.uk/campaigns/climate/issues/green_energy, or call 020 7490 1555. Mainstream suppliers' Green credentials are graded in the leaflet: by selecting one higher up the table you help shift the entire industry towards Greener energy.

Or try www.greenprices.com and www.uswitch.com 0845 601 2856, which have detailed information on green energy options. Simplest of all, switch to Unit-E, which provides energy from renewable sources all over Europe www.unit-e.co.uk (0845 601 1410), or Juice, a joint initiative from Greenpeace and npower. Visit www.npower.com/juice, or call 0800 389 2388.

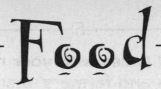

Food

1

Re-think your food –
you are what you eat!

Food is one of the greatest pleasures – a creative, social experience.
But all this has changed radically in the past few decades. The variety
and availability of produce has grown exponentially, our tastes have
become more diverse and the number of food outlets has rocketed.
But for all this convenience, we've sacrificed flavour and quality.

Recently, the nightmares of foot and mouth disease and BSE have
highlighted what we have lost in our race to be able to eat any food
we desire, whenever we choose. Farming is in crisis. People, and
especially children, have next to no understanding of where their food
comes from, how it is produced, or what it went through to get to
their plate. Artificially boosted foods have made it harder and harder
for us to appreciate the benefits of pure food, so hooked are we on
the sugar/salt/taste quick-fix.

It needn't be like this. Pockets of resistance are cropping up
everywhere, and people are becoming increasingly aware and
concerned about what they eat.

Buy locally produced food, from local shops and farmers' markets

By buying locally you support your own community and its economy and help reduce the massive and unnecessary CO_2 emissions from food transportation. In 1996, the UK imported 434,000 tonnes of apples, 202,000 tonnes of which were from outside the EU. The distribution of 1 kilogramme of apples from New Zealand creates its own weight in CO_2 emissions. Meanwhile, over 60% of UK apple orchards have been lost since 1970. Contact the National Association of Farmers' Markets at www.farmersmarkets.net.

3

Buy fruit and vegetables when they are in season

All fruits and vegetables have seasonal lifecycles – vast swathes of land on the other side of the world have been deprived of growing the crops their people need, so that instead they can produce the mange tout for our roasts and the satsumas for our summers. Having given up their land to produce export crops, the farmers are then forced to spend the money they earn growing crops they don't eat, just to buy back the crops they once grew for free.

'The Government needs to do something about its immigration policies!'

4

Buy Fair Trade bananas

The social and environmental costs of producing bananas are huge: 20% of Costa Rican male banana workers have been left sterile after handling toxic agri-chemicals, while women workers suffer double the national rate of leukaemia. Buy Fair Trade bananas (available in most supermarkets) and you'll know the farmer has received a fair price and working conditions. Other Fair Trade foods include coffee, tea, sugar, chocolate, orange juice and honey. Contact the Fair Trade Foundation at www.fairtrade.org.uk, or call 020 7405 5942.

5

Go without meat for a week

Meat production consumes vast amounts of resources – 10,000 litres of water are needed just to produce one kilogramme of beef, compared with only 500 litres of water needed to produce one kilogramme of potatoes. The less meat we as a population eat, the better the conditions under which the animals are reared will become. Go without meat for a week and see how many other options there are. Go to Compassion in World Farming to find out more www.ciwf.org, or call 01730 264 208.

6

Choose natural dieting methods

There are several types of food which actually help clear your cells of fat. Figs are rich in cellulose and hemicellulose, that absorb water and pick up fat as it passes through the body; apples and berries contain pectin, that frees cells of fat shortly after eating; and the vitamin C in citrus fruit alerts and stimulates the metabolic system, cleansing away accumulated fats. By contrast, aspartame, the most common artificial sweetener used in diet foods, is a known neurotoxin that has been linked to headaches, mood alterations and seizures.

7

Fight the GM giants!

Genetic engineering involves taking the genes from one species and inserting them into another to give it certain new qualities, such as improved resistance to cold weather conditions. There is a risk that genes engineered in plants and animals will be transferred to other species in the wild, causing irreversible damage to ecosystems. Genetically modified crops are driven by profits, not by the need to provide food to hungry populations as their manufacturers claim. An invaluable source of information is the Norfolk Genetic Information Network at www.ngin.org.uk. Try also The Organic Consumers Association at www.purefood.org and Totnes Genetics Group at www.togg.org.uk (01803 8400098).

Furniture and household appliances

1

Cut down on clutter!

It's easy to think another piece of furniture will help make the house more cosy, but sometimes the more clutter we fill the house with, the less space is left for ourselves! The furnishing business is a massive industry that doesn't always take into account that our home environment should be in harmony with our wider environment. When you're buying furniture, think about where it has come from and what processes it as gone through to get to your home.

'The washing machine is very energy efficient.
I just wish Frank was!'

Hang your clothes up to dry instead of using the tumble dryer

Tumble dryers are the most energy-consuming appliances we use in the home. If you do buy a tumble dryer, remember that gas appliances cost half as much to run as electric ones and produce 33% less greenhouse gas.

3

Recycle your curtains and old furniture

Curtains are resource-intensive in the amount of material they require – so don't leave them to fester in the garage or dump them in the rubbish. When you decide to change your curtains, get in touch with the Curtain Exchange at www.curtainexchange.net, which will buy your old curtains to make new ones. Otherwise, find your nearest textile recycler at www.wastepoint.co.uk/wasteconnect or call 01686 640 600. When you have old furniture, contact the Furniture Recycling Network at www.btinternet.com/~frn/FRN. For office furniture look in the Yellow Pages for recycling schemes.

4

Don't buy furniture that contains brominated flame retardants

Brominated flame retardants are a group of chemicals used in fabrics and plastics to counteract the spread of fires. They contribute to indoor air pollution and build up in the environment because they don't biodegrade. Several of them are also proven to be hormone disrupters, interfering with the daily functioning of the body. Some major furniture suppliers such as IKEA have stopped using them, but always check the company's policy when you buy new furniture.

Go M·A·D!

5
Buy energy-efficient white goods

Every year, UK households spend £800 million on electricity to run washing machines, tumble dryers and dishwashers – but by changing to more energy-efficient models you can save 33% on electricity bills. White goods now come with a rating from A to G, A being the most efficient, so look for the symbol when you are buying a white appliance.

6
Go for natural flooring

Carpets hide a number of unseen evils. The carpet, as well as its underlying pads and glues, can release formaldehyde, a known carcinogen, into the air for months or even years. Carpets are also a haven for house-dust mites that aggravate asthma. Most cleaning products for carpeting contain solvents and glycol ethers that may cause irritation and coughing when inhaled.

7
Never buy wooden furniture which comes from old-growth forests

Over 78% of the world's original old-growth forests have already been logged or degraded. Ask the retailer where the wood comes from and whether it comes from a sustainable source. Consumer pressure DOES work. In 1991, Friends of the Earth launched a campaign against the stocking of 'unsustainably-sourced' tropical timber by the 'big six' DIY chains. The campaign became a consumer boycott and by June 1994, all six had agreed to stop selling mahogany. Mahogany imports fell 68% by 1996. Contact the Rainforest Action Network to find specific campaigns against companies which are destroying our rainforests at www.ran.org. They also have information on how to buy alternatives to old-growth wood at www.ran.org/ran_campaigns/old_growth/alternatives.html.

Gardening

Think of your garden as an ecosystem

Your garden is an ecosystem teeming with life; and just as it contains its own micro-ecosystems, it is also part of the ecosystem of the surrounding area. Encourage biodiversity, by thinking about what species you plant and about the materials you use in your garden. Where do they come from, how were they made and what knock-on effects do they have? And have a break from tasteless mass-produced food – grow your own! Then you can guarantee it will be pesticide-free and hasn't been transported thousands of miles to reach your table. You don't need a garden to grow things... think window boxes, grow-bags, allotments, or just fill your bathroom with plants.

Contact the Wildlife Trusts for a leaflet on Wildlife Gardening by calling 01636 677 711, or going to www.wildlifetrusts.org.uk. And get in touch with the Henry Doubleday Research Foundation, a mine of information on gardening methods. Visit www.hdra.org.uk for good books to buy and for 'grow your own' information, or call 0247 630 3517.

2
KIDS – grow your own herbs

Whether you have a window box or a garden, growing your own herbs couldn't be easier. Not only will you have fresh herbs to add to your cooking and salads, but it's a lot cheaper and saves on packaging too!

3
Build homes for wildlife: install nesting boxes for bats and birds

The population of each of the 14 species of bat in Britain has declined in recent decades. The number of pipistrelle bats, for example, fell by 60% between 1978 and 1986. This reduction is caused by both the use of harmful pesticides and a decline in nesting places, as modern housing replaces old buildings with nooks and crannies for bats to roost in. Small garden birds are also threatened by a loss of habitat. When you install nesting boxes, make sure that they face away from direct sunlight and are out of reach of prowling cats. Contact the Bat Conservation Trust at www.bats.org.uk (020 7627 2629) or your nearest Wildlife Trust at www.wildlifetrusts.org.uk (01636 677 711) for more details.

4
Don't use a fuel-powered lawnmower

One fuel mower produces as much pollution in one hour as 40 cars. Use an electric mower instead. And bear in mind that grass is not always Greener anyway. Grass needs a lot more water and treatment against weeds than other hardier ground covers, and the more ground area covered by grass, the less area available for other species. Devote a larger area of your garden to other types of habitat such as a rockery, flowerbeds, a wild area or a vegetable patch.

Go M·A·D!

5

Don't treat fencing with creosote. Why have fences anyway? Go MAD with your borders!

Breathing in creosote fumes irritates the windpipe, and if it gets into food or drinking water it can cause burning in the mouth, stomach pains, convulsions and kidney problems. Creosote dissolves in water and can then get through the soil to groundwater, where it takes years for it to break down. Why not create a hedge or tree border instead, or build a wall from old bricks with crevices that can become a home to plants, insects and beetles? Old brick walls are a haven for wildlife and can also support a variety of species of creeper.

6

Avoid using water-worn limestone in your garden

The British Isles hold the world's most significant areas of limestone pavement, of which only 3% has escaped damage caused by man. It has been sculpted by glaciers and weathered for over 10,000 years resulting in a unique splintered appearance, with fissures that are home to rare plants, snails and butterflies. Water-worn limestone, used in rockeries, is also known as Irish limestone, Cumbrian stone or weathered limestone. There are several alternatives – sandstone, granite deep-quarried limestone, or York stone, as well as re-constituted and artificial substitutes made from fibreglass or cement.

7

Save our allotments!

Allotments are a vital breathing space in city areas and give people who have no access to gardens a chance to develop green fingers. Over the past two decades there has been a 43% drop in the number of allotments in the UK. The National Society of Allotment and Leisure Gardens campaigns to protect allotments from development. Find out about their work and get involved at www.nsalg.co.uk or call 01536 266 576. The Wavendon Allotment and Garden Society has a database of allotment sites around the UK. Visit www.btinternet.com/~cbownes/wags, or call 01908 586095.

Glass

'I want to come back as a decanter next time!'

1

Get down to the bottle-bank!

◆

Glass is much better for the environment as a packaging material than plastic, because there is no shortage of the materials used to make it (sand, soda ash and limestone as opposed to crude oil) and its manufacture causes less pollution. But these materials still have to be mined, creating scars on the landscape.

Recycling glass reduces the amount of raw materials used by 80% and uses 22% less energy than starting from scratch. Glass can be recycled indefinitely as its structure does not deteriorate when it's reprocessed. But despite the fact that there are 20,000 bottle banks in the UK we still only recycle 25% of our glass bottles and jars. The European average is 50% and some countries manage more than 80% so we have a lot of catching up to do!

KIDS – paint old jars and bottles to give as presents

You don't have to be an artist to transform a jar into an attractive, personal present with glass paints that come in striking colours. You can buy glass paints in most good art shops - choose organic whenever possible!

Make your own, environmentally friendly glass cleaner

Most commercial glass cleaners contain isopropyl alcohol – a strong chemical that kills aquatic life when it gets into river water and is a potential nervous system depressant. Instead of using commercial glass cleaners, mix a tablespoonful of vinegar with a pint of water.

Recycle all of your waste glass

Recycling just one glass bottle saves enough energy to power a TV set for an hour and a half. The 600,000 tonnes of glass recycled in the UK last year saved enough energy to power every primary school in the UK for a year. For every tonne of glass recycled a saving of 135 litres of oil and 1.2 tonnes of ash, sand and limestone is made. If we recycled all our glass we could save four times this amount of energy and resources. Go to www.recycle-more.co.uk to find your nearest bottle bank.

Go M·A·D!

————————— 5 —————————

Make work easier for glass recyclers

The glass recycling process depends on the glass not being 'contaminated' by products other than glass and on the separation of different coloured glass. Put different coloured bottles in the right bank and remove metal or plastic tops, corks and rings from bottles or jars. Light bulbs, cookware such as 'pyrex' or 'visionware' and flat glass, such as window glass, should not be put in bottle banks. Find out what to do with these types of glass from British Glass www.britglass.co.uk (follow links to 'glass recycling' then 'glass recycling code'), or call 0114 268 6201. Also, visit www.wastepoint.co.uk/wasteconnect and www.recycle-more.co.uk.

————————— 6 —————————

Recycle old spectacles

There are thousands of people in the developing world who are handicapped by short sight because they cannot afford or don't have access to glasses. Next time you get a new pair of glasses, take your old pair to be recycled. Vision Aid Overseas is a nationwide scheme that sets up eye clinics in developing countries and supplies patients with second-hand spectacles. Many local opticians collect spectacles for Vision Aid – if yours doesn't, tell them about the scheme, and meanwhile you can send old spectacles to Vision Aid by post. Find out more at www.vao.org.uk, or call 01259 353 5016.

————————— 7 —————————

Campaign for a kerbside collection to be set up in your local area

Councils have been good at setting up collection schemes for paper but are slower on the uptake when it comes to collecting your glass. A collection scheme means that twice as many people will recycle their glass than if they had to take it to a bottle bank. It also means less pollution and traffic from all the saved journeys to the bottle bank.

Go wild

'Isn't Bill going a little TOO wild?'

1

Other creatures live here too

The UK is a crowded country. 60 million people are busy making the landscape more 'human', and in the meantime destroying the habitats and livelihoods of many millions of other creatures.

Since 1945, we have lost an estimated 95% of flower-rich meadows, 30% of ancient woodland and 80% of lowland grassland in the UK. As it disappears, so our fellow creatures are being done out of places to live. For those living in cities it's all too easy to forget we share our country with thousands of other species. But just because we cannot see them, they are still there, and all the litter, noise and pollution we make is still felt by them. We all want a world filled with nature's treasures, but are we willing to look after it?

KIDS – don't feed milk to hedgehogs

75% of hedgehogs in the UK die before they are one year old. At least 100,000 are killed on the roads, and 5,000 are killed by gamekeepers who mistakenly think they are 'vermin' that eat the eggs of nesting birds. Hedgehogs need all the help they can get to survive, but don't give them milk. Hedgehogs cannot digest milk and it gives them severe diarrhoea, which leads to dehydration and death within a couple of days. Instead, offer them a nightly dish of tinned cat or dog food or any meaty leftovers from your meals. They also like digestive biscuits. Find out more about hedgehogs and how you can help them from the Hedgehog Preservation Society at www.hedgehogs.org.uk, or call 01202 699 358.

— 3 —

Pick up those fag butts!

Most smokers are aware of the risk of fire when they drop cigarette butts so they make sure that they stamp them out. What they are less aware of is the threat to small birds and animals. The foam filter of cigarettes chokes small creatures, and if they do manage to swallow them they are poisoned by the tobacco and tar. So pick them up!

— 4 —

Don't drop litter. It can kill

Last year the RSPCA rescued 7,063 animals due to litter-related injuries – a massive increase of 23.5% on the previous year. The casualties included a young goose with a fishing hook in its eye, a hedgehog trapped inside a plastic drinks bottle and a sheep with a child's plastic chair stuck over its head. Ouch!

Go M·A·D!

Help bring our butterflies back

Five of the 59 butterfly species known to have bred in the UK have become extinct, the most recent being the large blue and the large tortoiseshell. Several others are at critical level, such as the high brown fritillary that has declined by over 94% since the 1950s, and eleven moth species have become extinct in the last century. Contact Butterfly Conservation to find out what plants you can grow in your garden to encourage butterflies, and how you can get involved in your local group. Visit www.butterfly-conservation.org.uk or call 01929 400 209.

6

Give an owl a home

Owls depend on hollow trees or cosy corners of old buildings and barns to make their homes. With spreading modern developments they often find themselves homeless. But whatever part of the country you live in, you can provide an owl with a home. Tawny owls will take up residence in nest boxes in the smallest gardens in urban areas, while barn owls will move into boxes installed on more isolated land. If you don't have space, you can 'adopt' an owl box (this is popular with Brownies!). Find out more about this and installing owl boxes from the Hawk and Owl Trust at www.hawkandowl.org or call 01582 832 182.

7

Stamp out illegal wildlife trade

The illegal trade in wildlife is second only to the narcotics trade in terms of size and value. From the hunting of dolphins to the illegal logging of the rainforest and bear-baiting, the Environmental Investigation Agency carries out undercover investigations to expose the horrific treatment we inflict on animals across the world. And not only to expose it, but also put an end to it. For eye-opening reports on EIAs exposures, its campaigns and how you can help, contact them at www.eia-international.org, or call 020 7354 7960.

─Health─

Keep healthy by creating a healthy environment

We are constantly being informed of how much healthier a society we live in now than in the past. We do indeed live longer, and certain diseases have been eradicated (though some, such as TB, are beginning to make a comeback). But we have given up a great deal in getting here. By relying on pills and potions and entrusting everything to the professionals, we have surrendered control and understanding of our own bodies.

We now reach for the pills or call the doctor the moment we feel the slightest chill or headache. But there is nothing wrong with being mildly ill, and our body is the best doctor and dispensary we have. Be wary, too, of the fact that drugs companies are always ready to cash in on the latest 'syndrome'.

'Now, wait a second....
it's i before e, except after c...'

KIDS – eat five pieces of fruit and veg a day

Eating five pieces of fruit a day protects you against coronary heart disease and some cancers, but people in the UK eat far less fruit and veg than other countries in Europe. Fruit and veg also provide you with essential minerals and vitamins which are not available in other foods. Find out about Sustain's Grab 5 campaign at www.sustainweb.org/fruitandveg/backgr.htm (020 7837 1228) and encourage your school to take part in Grab 5's activities such as breakfast clubs, playground markets and classroom games.

3

Open the window

Humans are outdoor creatures, just like any other species. But we now spend at least 80% of our time indoors. The Environmental Protection Agency has found that indoor air quality is often five times worse and can be up to 100 times worse than the air outdoors. People are increasingly linking ill-health, even cancers, to the state of the environment and the air we breathe: indoors, bad air builds up as a result of fungi and bacteria, hazardous building materials, furnishings that give off carcinogenic chemicals, or gas heaters and stoves that release carbon monoxide. So if you do have to spend a lot of time indoors, keep the fresh air circulating.

4

Support your local pharmacy

Price cuts in supermarket medicine prices have threatened the future of 12,000 local pharmacies, which are essential to the well-being of a local community. Groups that will be particularly affected by their loss are the elderly, disabled and young mothers, who rely heavily on the free advice and range of services offered by local pharmacies. When the pharmacies go, you will have no choice but to go to the supermarket for medicines.

Look at all the alternatives

Your GP is not the only professional out there able to keep you healthy. Osteopathy, yoga, acupuncture, Tai Chi and homeopathy, to name but a few, all provide long-lasting and rewarding paths to health. And while most of the solutions your doctor prescribes will only address the specific problem that you have gone to see them about, alternative medicines take a holistic view of your health. The Complementary Medicine Association is a good place to start, visit www.the-cma.org.uk, or call 020 8305 9571.

—— *6* ——

Have regular cancer check ups and learn to check yourself

1,200 women die from cervical cancer each year, but this figure would be 4,000 higher if regular smear tests did not take place. A smear test can never be 100% perfect, but non-attendance at smear tests is still the biggest risk-factor in contracting cervical cancer – half of cases are among those who have not had a test (15% of women have not had a smear test in the past five years). 1,500 men each year develop testicular cancer in the UK and it is the single biggest cause of cancer-related deaths in men aged 15-35 in the UK. But the main worry is that the number of UK cases has trebled in the past 25 years and is still rising. Find out how to check for signs at www.netdoctor.co.uk/diseases/facts/testicularcancer.htm.

—— *7* ——

Give the poor a chance

In developing countries, 30,000 people a day die because effective medicines are too expensive or just not available. Now, the World Trade Organisation's Trade Related Aspects of Intellectual Property Rights – Trips – has set a worldwide standard for protecting patents, including medicines. As multinational drugs companies hold over 90% of drugs patents they effectively have control over the global market in drugs. Help Oxfam's Cut the Cost campaign in petitioning the WTO to reform Trips, so that third world governments have the right to obtain the cheapest possible life-saving medicines without facing the threats of legal challenges or trade sanctions. Sign the global petition at www.oxfam.org.uk/cutthecost. For more information about TRIPs, visit Tradewatch at www.citizen.org.

Heating

1

Turn down the heat!

◆

Everyone wants to be warm and comfortable in their home. While turning the thermostat up a couple of notches may solve the problem in the short term, it is not the ultimate solution. Despite what some of the oil industry might have you believe, global warming is not a good thing – nor a solution to being cold! The prospect of some nicer summers for a few years won't be worth the price.

The good news is that you don't have to sacrifice heat in the home to keep the world cool. A few simple steps can not only help save the planet, but they can save you money in the long run too – half of our energy bills go towards heating our homes and water supply.

'They've got insulation to die for!'

Turn down your thermostat by 1°C

For every degree that you turn down your thermostat by you will save approximately 10% on your heating bill and cut down on greenhouse gas emissions. If you feel chilly, put on an extra layer of clothing!

―――――― 3 ――――――

Fit aluminium foil behind radiators

This reflects the heat back into the room and will save you £10 per year, per radiator. You can also save a lot of energy by heating only the rooms you need to use. Heating control devices and thermostatic radiator valves enable you to control the temperature of each room separately, and a timeswitch will turn your heating and hot water on and off automatically at the times you set.

―――――― 4 ――――――

Insulate!

More than 50% of the heat lost from your home is through loft spaces and walls: if you install a layer of insulation 20cm thick in the loft you can save 20% of your heating costs, and cavity wall insulation can cut heat loss through the wall by up to 60%. There are three types of insulation. Greenest first, they are: organic (from natural vegetation and renewable resources); inorganic (derived from minerals, for example fibreglass, loose fill and foamed glass); and fossil organic (derived from the chemical industry, for example expanded polystyrene). The Centre for Alternative Energy can advise you on different types of insulating material and where you can buy them. Visit www.cat.org.uk, or call 01654 702 400.

If your central heating system packs up replace it with a condensing boiler

Condensing boilers are the most efficient type of boiler, converting 88% of fuel into heat compared with 72% for standard boilers, and they save an extra 12% on heating costs. They contain an extra heat exchanger: the hot exhaust gases use much of their energy to pre-heat the water in the boiler system, and when the boiler works at peak efficiency the water vapour produced in the combustion process condenses back into liquid releasing extra heat. Find out more about them at www.natenergy.org.uk/boiler.htm or call the National Energy Foundation's free helpline on 0800 512 012.

—————————— *6* ——————————

Go SOLAR!

On a cloudy day in Britain a solar roof can generate enough electricity to play 70 episodes of Coronation Street and make 35 cups of tea. A one-kilowatt solar panel can save a tonne of CO_2 emissions each year. Contact the National Energy Foundation's renewable energy pages at www.greenenergy.org.uk or the Centre for Alternative Energy at www.cat.org.uk (01654 702 400) for details.

—————————— *7* ——————————

Give your house a heating makeover!

Every house is different and some energy-saving devices may be better for your home than others. There are currently over 50 Energy Efficiency Advice centres across the UK that offer free independent advice on how you can make your home more efficient, especially through regulating its heating. Find your nearest one via the National Energy Foundation at www.natenergy.co.uk, or call 0800 512 012. Or contact Energy Saving Installers on 0845 727 7200 who will put you in touch with a local installer to advise you on the best energy efficiency options to suit your needs.

Hotels

1

Stand out from the crowd

◆

You've worked hard all year. You need a rest. No wonder the all-inclusive hotel complex with jacuzzi, dinner, wine and traditional native dance thrown in looks so appealing. But while it may seem like an easy option, is it really the best place to stay, for you or for the people in the place you are visiting?

Where is the sense of adventure, the discovery of places unknown, the encounter with people unlike ourselves? In a chain hotel, one place is much like another...

'Darling, remind me again – which country are we in?'

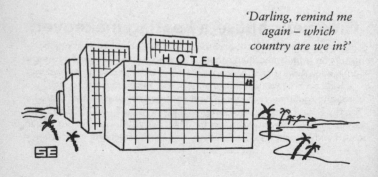

Conserve water when you're in countries with limited supplies

The average tourist uses as much water in 24 hours as a third world villager uses in 100 days. Encourage hotels to conserve water by installing low-flow showerheads, sink aerators and toilets. Tank-fill diverters in older toilets can save 4 litres of water for every flush.

3

Avoid all-inclusive hotel complexes

All inclusive for you – exclusive from the local economy. Tourists who stay in an all-inclusive hotel leave their wallet at home so, apart from the local people who are employed by the complex, none of their money will filter into the local community. They also make swathes of land, often in the most beautiful parts of the country, inaccessible to the local population. Half the UK visitors to the Caribbean each year stay in an all-inclusive resort and the sector is growing by 22% a year.

4

Always think local

Use local tour operators, stay in locally-run hotels and only buy local goods. A study of tourism 'leakage' in Thailand estimated that 70% of all money spent by tourists ended up leaving Thailand, via hotels, tour operators, airlines and imported food and drink. For travel choices which emphasise local food, environmental concerns and unique experiences, try the *Special Places to Stay* series by Sawdays. Go to www.sawdays.co.uk or call 01275 464891.

Go M·A·D!

5

Ask your hotel to put 're-use' towel and sheet cards in the bedroom and bathroom

Few guests mind using their sheets or towels for more than one day – if each room has signs that people can use to tell the chamber maid they don't mind using their sheets or towels again hotels will cut at least 5% off their energy use. The likelihood is that 70% of guests will choose to reuse.

6

Don't use the freebie 'mini' soaps and shampoos

Hotels could save on thousands of bags of waste by using refillable dispensers for shampoo and skincare, and by recycling soap. Don't encourage their use of mini bottles and containers that cause unnecessary waste of resources and energy in their production.

7

Look out for the Green Globe sign

Green Globe 21 was set up by the World Travel and Tourism Council following the Rio Earth Summit in 1992, and gives certification to hotels, as well as airlines and travel agents, which meet their environmental standards. Their website www.greenglobe21.com has a list of all their members, in 100 countries worldwide, or you can call 01892 541 717.

The American organisation Green Hotels has useful Green tips for hotels that you can bear in mind when staying in them. It also has member hotels in America, Canada, Central and South America. Visit www.greenhotels.com.

Hygiene

1

Re-think what clean means

Aggressive marketing shouts out at us everywhere we look, promoting a supposedly cleaner lifestyle. Everything can now be brighter than bright, whiter than white, and smell of pine forests along the way. However, the products we use to create this illusion of purity do so by damaging the environment we live in. This takes place at every stage of their lifecycle – the manufacturing process pollutes, their usage gives off harmful chemicals into the atmosphere, and when they are disposed of they are rarely recycled.

Take off your shoes indoors

Household carpet dust can contain 30 different toxic chemicals, and pesticide levels up to 50 times higher than in nearby soil samples. When you whip round with the vacuum cleaner, most of these residues cling on tight to the carpet, building up over the years. They are mainly brought in on the soles of shoes, so taking them off is the first step towards making your house as clean as you'd like to believe it is!

Buy recycled toilet paper and only use two sheets at a time

Each person in the UK now uses 16.8 rolls of toilet tissue each year: that's a mammoth 60 square metres, and is a two-roll increase on the figure for 1999 (is that because we are going to the toilet more often? – unlikely!). The amount of Andrex sold in a year is enough to go round the M25 80,000 times. While the paper used for toilet rolls may come from sustainably managed forests, these forests, mainly conifer, are replacing ancient woodland in Scandinavia that is home to thousands of endangered species.

Use natural soaps

Commercial soaps often contain the strong degreasing agent sodium laurel sulphate or sodium laureth sulphate, a potent chemical that can destroy delicate tissues in the eye and skin. Not to mention all the artificial fragrances and colours. Contact Simply Soaps at www.simplysoaps.com or call 0775 564 802.

Never use an aerosol

Although they no longer contain ozone depleting CFCs, many still contain hydrocarbon propellants that contribute to air pollution and when inhaled, irritate the lungs.

———————— 6 ————————

Avoid deodorants containing aluminium

Most commercial deodorants contain either aluminium chlorohydrate or aluminium zirconium, both of which are easily absorbed into the skin. Once in the body, the aluminium passes across cell membranes and is absorbed by the liver, kidney, brain, cartilage and bone marrow – increasing the risk of blood poisoning. Aluminium-containing antiperspirants also block our pores to stop us from sweating. For the kindest deodorant to the environment buy a deodorant stone, which is free from aluminium chlorohydrate and is based on natural mineral salts. Go to www.deodorant-stone.co.uk, or call 01666 826 515.

———————— 7 ————————

Swap to non-bleached sanitary products

A big step when we're so used to the easy-to-use sanitary products on the shop shelves. In just 40 years, women have been convinced that bleached disposable pads and tampons are the only acceptable option – without taking into account the possible health risks. Due to the fact that a woman may use as many as 11,000 tampons in her lifetime she is exposed to extra levels of dioxin, the by-product of chlorine bleaching. Dioxin has been linked to cancers and immune system depression. Tampons also have additives to increase absorbency such as surfactants that may also pose health risks. But you can avoid these risks with non-chlorine-bleached sanitary products. Also ask your doctor about the risks of toxic shock syndrome, that can be caused by tampons. Find out more about non-bleached products from the Spirit of Nature at www.spiritofnature.co.uk, or call 0870 725 9885.

Go M·A·D!

Investment

1

Invest in the environment!

◆

You don't have to be a shareholder to have an investment in a company. If you have a pension, a mortgage, insurance or just a bank account, the money you spend is being invested for you. Without realising it, your money could be filtering into the arms trade, companies that employ children or contaminate the water supply of their local population.

Investment also gives you the power to stop these things happening. Over the past few years, people have become increasingly aware that, despite the claims in their advertising, not all companies are whiter than white. As a result, opportunities to direct where your money goes and to influence the decision-making powers of those who spend it has never been higher on the agenda.

Bank your principles

Switch your current account to an ethical bank such as the Co-operative Bank – see www.co-operativebank.co.uk, or call 0161 832 3456. For your deposit account, try the Triodos Bank. Visit www.triodos.co.uk, or call 0117 973 9339. Some banks contribute to developing countries' burden of debt, to the manufacture or distribution of arms, or to oppressive regimes by encouraging trade with them. Ethical banks not only avoid such forms of investment, but also discriminate in favour of companies with good environmental policies. And if you do change, remember to let your old bank know why.

3

Choose green insurance

When you join the AA or the RAC you are indirectly giving support to the bulldozing of the countryside for more roads, because these organisations lobby the government to increase road building. By choosing the Environmental Transport Association as your insurer you will be supporting an organisation that campaigns for alternative methods of transport and a reduction in car use, while recognising our need for cars. Visit www.eta.org or call them on 01932 828 882. For ethical household, house contents or travel insurance, contact Naturesave Policies Ltd at www.naturesave.co.uk, or call 01803 864 390

4

Make it good to talk

Sign up to the Phone Co-op. Half of the Phone-Co-op's profits are pooled into a fund to which charities and voluntary organisations apply for grants. They are aiming to cut out all the CO_2 emissions caused by their members' phone calls and the running of the company. Furthermore, you could cut your bills by up to 80%. Visit www.phonecoop.org.uk or call 0845458 9000 for more details.

Go M·A·D!

5

Take out a green mortgage

People are usually less concerned about who they are borrowing from than who they invest in, and tend not to worry about the policies of building societies because they believe they only have housing investments – but many of the older building societies are now more like banks in their lending policies. The Co-operative Bank (www.co-operativebank.co.uk, or call 0161 832 3456) and the Norwich and Peterborough Building Society (www.norwichandpeterborough.co.uk, or call 0845 300 6727) offer mortgage products linked to reforestation schemes. The Ecology Building Society is a Green building society that provides mortgages for properties which give an ecological payback. Find out more at www.ecology.co.uk, or call 0845 674 5566.

6

Retire ethically!

Pension funds control more than a third of the shares in the UK stock market – and everybody with a pension fund is responsible for ensuring that their money is ethically invested. Look at your pension fund's Statement of Investment Principles, which may be sent to you automatically – if not – request it. If the details of the ethical policy aren't clear, write back for a more detailed explanation.

7

Use your investor-power

Influence a company's policy-making by using your position as a direct shareholder to attend, vote, and speak at annual meetings of the company. And only invest in companies whose ethical principles match your own. Friends Provident's Stewardship Funds enable you to invest ethically by selecting companies which have a positive ecological impact. Contact them at www.friendsprovident.co.uk, or call on 0870 600 6300.

The Ethical Investment Research Service (EIRIS) has a database of over 2,000 companies and their policies, and can tailor-make 'acceptable lists' for individuals, of the companies that most fit their ethical concerns. EIRIS has found that investment along ethical lines does not have to mean a reduction in returns! Visit www.eiris.org, or call 020 7840 5700.

—Keep cool—

1

Keeping cool is a costly business – both for you and the environment

Fridges are an everyday part of our lives, but as they hum gently in the background, they're doing a vast amount of damage to the environment.

Refrigeration and freezing appliances in UK homes use as much electricity as the total amount used by offices, accounting for 36% of all the energy consumed by electrical appliances in the UK. But it's not only the energy consumption that harms the environment. CFCs – which were shown to be harmful to the ozone layer – have now been replaced in some refrigeration equipment by HCFCs and HFCs. Although these are not 'ozone depleting' gases, they still make a significant contribution to the greenhouse effect – their chlorine content makes them hundreds of times more harmful than CO_2. It's almost impossible to imagine life without fridges and freezers. But there are plenty of actions you can take to whittle down their harmful effect.

Keep your fridge between 3-5°C

Fridges don't need to be any cooler than 3°C – if they are, they are wasting energy. Keeping a thermometer in the fridge will help you make sure the temperature never falls below 3°C.

— *3* —

Keep the coils at the back of your fridge free from dust

When dust accumulates on the condenser coils, energy consumption can increase by 30%.

— *4* —

Buy a fridge-saver plug

A saver plug works on the basis that when a fridge is running its compressor is not fully loaded all the time – the plug senses these times and cuts out power to the motor in rapid short bursts without changing the operation of the fridge. This can reduce the energy used by the fridge by over 20%, giving you a return of £140 over 10 years. Visit www.savawatt.com/savaplug.htm.

— *5* —

Make sure your fridge is free-standing and in a cool environment

That way it operates most efficiently. Putting cooked food that is still warm into the fridge also makes it less efficient.

Go M·A·D!

6

Never dump your old fridge – take it to be safely recycled

Three million fridges are scrapped in the UK each year, containing
2000 tonnes of CFCs or HCFCs. Some local authorities do provide a
coolant removing service, but only 15% of coolant is currently
removed. So make sure you take your old fridge to a recycling point
that can deal with it safely. Find your nearest one at
www.wastepoint.co.uk/wasteconnect or call 0800 435576.

7

Now cool it!

Get a 100% ozone-friendly fridge. 'Greenfreeze' fridges are now
widely available. They work on a mixture of propane and butane, and
contain no CFCs, HFCs, or HCFCs.
Also when you buy a fridge, make sure it's energy-efficient. An
energy-efficient fridge uses up to 70% less energy – they cost £50
more but within 18 months you will have made back the extra through
cheaper running costs. Look for the energy consumption ratings that
now have to be displayed on all models: They are graded from A
(most efficient) down to G (least efficient).

Contact the Energy+ project for more information. It brings together
retailers and European institutions to promote the most energy-
efficient fridge-freezers on the market: visit www.energy-plus.org, or
call 01865 281 123.

—Lighting—

*'I often get the feeling that
I'm going to die young.'*

---------- 1 ----------

Brighter lights don't make a brighter world

Every year, UK households spend a total of £1.2 billion on electricity for lighting.

But because we take it for granted it's easy to forget the effect our lighting has on the environment. Lighting is responsible for 7% of CO_2 emissions in the UK, and 16% of our domestic electricity use. We can dramatically reduce consumption simply by switching lights off every time we leave a room, not sleeping with the light on, and waiting an extra 20 minutes before we turn our lights on in the evenings.

Be a glow-worm. Generate your own light with a clockwork torch

By winding up your clockwork torch you recharge its battery – so effectively it will provide endless light without you ever having to buy a new one. Clockwork torches are catching on and will help light the lives of many people in developing countries – for free. Clockwork torches are manufactured by BayGen and can be bought in most large travel shops.

3

Switch to energy-efficient light bulbs

One unit of electricity supplied to a customer can provide the same amount of light for 10 hours or 40 hours for exactly the same price, depending on the type of bulb you use. Compact fluorescent lightbulbs (CFLs) use 70% less electricity than traditional incandescent or halogen lights and last ten times longer. If every household swapped to energy-efficient bulbs it would save enough energy to power the lighting used in two million homes for a year. They cost about £10 each but over their 10,000 hour lifetime an 11-Watt bulb saves £35 and a 20-Watt bulb saves £57.

4

Fill your house with sunlight

A great way to make the most of natural light is to paint your walls a light colour so you'll need less artificial light. Also, one skylight can bring enough light into a small room never to need electric lighting during the day. Natural sunlight is not only brighter than fluorescent light, but it doesn't distort colours, so your house will be filled with true, natural illumination. You can even buy a tube skylight that will direct sunlight from the roof through into a room. Find out more from Solalighting at www.solalighting.com, or call 0845 458 0101.

Don't use bright halogen burglar detector lights on your property

48% of lighting complaints to local authorities are related to domestic security lights. The detector systems used for halogen lights are over-sensitive and rarely installed properly so detect roaming cats as well as burglars – they are usually over 150 Watts, wasting large amounts of electricity. Nor are they effective: their glare is so bright that shadows become darker, making it easier for intruders to hide, and because people become accustomed to their endless flashing, they are no longer alerted by the glare. Instead of halogen lights, install a low-power compact fluorescent lamp that is cheaper, more effective and gentler on the environment.

Sign your business up to Lightswitch

The Energy Savings Trust and the lighting industry have teamed up to help companies cut their lighting bills and help reduce global warming. Small companies (under 250 employees) often spend 30% of their electricity bill on lighting. Lightswitch will give rebates of up to £6,000 to help your company install energy efficient lighting. Visit www.lightswitch.co.uk, or call 08705 133 538.

Help put the stars back in the sky

Do you ever wonder where all the stars have gone? Light pollution has increased so dramatically over the past 40 years that in many large cities the stars are few and far between. Keep your eyes open for floodlights on advertising hoardings that are left on in the small hours of the morning, and for cloud spotlights above nightclubs, and report them to the local authority. The British Astronomical Society has set up a Campaign for Brighter Skies. Visit their website to find out more about good lighting, bad lighting, and how you can make a difference to the night sky at www.dark-skies.freeserve.co.uk. The International Dark-Sky Association has information on how to minimise light pollution by choosing the right light fittings. Visit www.darksky.org.

Go M·A·D!

L♂ve

1

GET (RE) CONNECTED

Since love makes the world go round and this is a book about the world, love deserves a mention. In a sense, all of these tips to Make A Difference are about love, in that they show you really care about the world you live in and the people with whom you share it.

At the moment the world needs our love more than ever. As most of us no longer live in close contact with the land, it's easy to forget how much we owe to it and how much we depend on its well-being for our survival. So instead we focus more on loving ourselves. Meanwhile, the world is being drained of its resources to satisfy our ever-increasing demands. If love is about connections between living beings, it should also be about re-enforcing the connections between us and the world we live in.

'I just love to hear an environmentalist talking dirty.'

2

KIDS – make a friend out of cress!

Take a small tray. Plant cress seeds in the shape of a friend's name, and give the tray to that friend. Tell them to water it regularly and wait. They'll be surprised when shoots start to spring up and spell their name - a perfect present to show you care about someone.

3

Find a Green mate

If you're looking for a partner, why not hunt for an environmental one and you can Make A Difference together... get in touch with a "Green" dating agency such as Natural Friends at www.natural-friends.com, or call 01284 728 315. Or if that seems a bit unsubtle, join a local environmental group. Friends of the Earth have groups across the country which meet to discuss and campaign together. Visit www.foe.org.uk or call 020 7490 1555.

4

Take a natural love drug

Pau de Reposta is a herbal aphrodisiac from Brazil. It works miracles by stimulating the sexual nervous system. It's used across the world as an effective treatment for male impotency, but is also used by healthy men and women to dramatically improve their sex drive. What are you waiting for?! If you want something less adventurous, try the classic 'aphrodisiac' foods - oysters or asparagus – organic, naturally!

Go M·A·D!

5

Give your loved one a plant on Valentine's day instead of roses – how about a rose bush?

The blossoming bunches of roses you buy in a florists have usually been cultivated in mass plantations the other side of the world, doused in pesticides and consumed vast quantities of water in locations where water is scarce. They're then transported thousands of miles to reach their point of sale.

6

Love little things!

Our senses are bombarded the whole time, but so much so that it's easy to forget to appreciate them, to forget quite how magical it can be to be alive. Spend a day noticing the smell of your food, the expressions on people's faces, the texture of objects, the changing light throughout the day.

7

Unite!

All over the world, people have achieved change through linking their voices together, whether it's halting plans for the construction of an incinerator, or saving a species from extinction. One of the biggest threats to the future of our planet is global warming - CO_2, the main heat-trapping gas, is at the highest levels the planet has seen for 20 million years. Link up with people planet-wide to turn the heat down before it's too late. ClimateArk is a great campaigning tool against global warming: visit www.climateark.org.

And for love in the 'peace and love' sense, festivals are it! Go MAD at Womad (World of Music Arts and Dance). The UK Womad festival usually takes place in early summer, but they are held all year round, all around the world, bringing together traditional arts groups and keeping cultural diversity alive. Find out all about it at www.womad.org, or call 01225 743188. For radical street-partying action contact Reclaim the Streets at www.reclaimthestreets.net (020 7281 4621). Festival Eye, a magazine and website, gives a comprehensive list of all festivals going on across the UK – visit www.festivaleye.com, or call 01568 760 492. Or try Efestival's website: www.efestivals.co.uk for music festival listings and reviews.

Marriage

1

Have a Green wedding!

The symbolism in traditional weddings implies that there are parallels between the union of two people and the union of those people with the earth. But now a wedding is more likely to cost the earth, than bring us closer to it.

Couples spend on average £14,000 on getting married. But if you want to stand out and be different on your wedding day, you don't have to follow the crowd and run up the same bill. A Green wedding saves not only your pocket but the environment, and it is no more difficult to arrange.

ALL MY LIFE I WANTED A WHITE WEDDING, THEN I GO AND GET INVOLVED WITH SOMEONE WHO WANTS A GREEN ONE!

Send your invitations on recycled or natural handmade paper

Recycled paper or handmade paper adds an original look to your invites. Recycled Paper Supplies will print invitations on recycled paper for you. Visit www.recycled-paper.co.uk, or call 01676 533 832.

Cut down on cars

Save the environment from the pollution of all those cars carrying just one or two people. Include clear directions in the invitation for how people can reach the wedding by public transport, and details of places for them to stay nearby. How about organising for a double-decker bus to pick up your guests from a central meeting point? Also try to have the ceremony and the reception within walking distance of each other.

Ask your guests to donate to your favourite charity

Instead of asking for presents, ask your friends and family to donate to your favourite charity, and make a lasting difference to the environment.

5

Make your own wedding cake

This way you can ensure that all the ingredients are organic and locally produced, and that the eggs are from organically fed free-range chickens. If you are having a meal or serving nibbles at the reception, try to use organic ingredients.

The Campaign for Real Food is a group of caterers providing freshly prepared food from natural ingredients and local produce wherever possible. Call 020 7771 0099. And for vegetarian or vegan caterers, call More Food For Thought on 020 7836 9072.

6

Entertain by candlelight

Candles add atmosphere as well as saving electricity. Use natural beeswax or vegetable-based candles that biodegrade and are smoke-free. Paraffin candles are made from petroleum residues, so do neither your health or the environment any good. Beeswax candles also last twice as long and burn brighter! And select locally produced or homegrown flowers.

7

Ride away on a tandem

No need for a plush Rolls-Royce when you could bring originality and romance into your wedding by leaving your guests on a tandem bicycle, and you won't be polluting the atmosphere. And how about making a difference on your honeymoon too? For good ideas visit Tourism Concern's Community Tourism Directory www.tourismconcern.org.uk/community/frame.htm.

Nappies

1

In the UK, we throw away nine million nappies a day – that's three billion a year!

Nappies are one of Britain's major waste problems. The average baby will get through a total of 5,840 of them. Disposable nappies account for 4% of landfill waste, where they can take 500 years to decompose, and there is also the risk that viruses from human faeces can seep into groundwater supplies. As many as 100 viruses can survive in soiled nappies for up to two weeks, including the live polio virus excreted by recently vaccinated babies.

It takes a cup of crude oil to produce the plastic for one disposable nappy and, in the UK alone, seven million trees are felled each year to produce wood pulp for disposable nappies.

Yet babies survived right up until the 1970s with cotton nappies. Why can't we all still use them now? They produce 60 times less solid waste than disposables. It's time to clean up our act.

Pins, too much hassle? Buy Velcro-fastening cotton nappies

Now you have no excuse. Companies such as Earthwise Baby www.earthwisebaby.com (01908 587 275) and Eco-Babes www.eco-babes.co.uk (01353 664 941) sell a range of easy-to-use cotton nappies.

─────────── *3* ───────────

Keep baby's bottom as dry as possible – and don't use moist tissue wipes

This reduces the baby's likelihood of contracting nappy-rash, a reaction to chemicals in the urine and faeces. And if you thought that cotton nappies meant a higher chance of nappy rash – WRONG! Research by the American Medical Association found that nappy rash occurs in 54% of babies using disposable nappies, and only 18% of babies using cloth nappies. Moist baby wipes are full of chemicals such as alcohol, preservatives, fragrances and moisturisers – babies' skin is even more sensitive to these artificial chemicals than yours.

─────────── *4* ───────────

If you must use disposables, buy eco-disposable nappies

Their manufacturing process does far less harm to the environment than that of normal disposables, not least because they don't contain bleaching agents. They are also free from perfumes and other chemicals which may harm your baby's skin.

5

Never flush a disposable
nappy down the toilet

The super-absorbent gel in disposable nappies absorbs water and the
nappies swell so much that they block pipes. Nappies which do get
through the sewerage system will eventually end up on our beaches.

6

Use a nappy washing service

Nappy services use 32% less energy than home washing, and 41% less
water. They also make life much easier for you. Contact the National
Association of Nappy Washing services to find out about services in
your area, visit www.changeanappy.co.uk, or call 0121 6934949.

WASHABLE

*'You're a menace
to the environment!'*

*'Yeah? You're
so full of crap!'*

*'Well at least it can
be washed out!'*

DISPOSABLE

7

Help make the change

Real Nappy Week is a nationwide campaign to get people to switch
from disposable to cotton. Get involved at www.realnappy.com, or call
01656 783 405. The Real Nappy Association will also tell you all you
need to know about cotton nappies, where to buy them and what to
consider when buying. Also visit The Nappy Lady
www.thenappylady.co.uk, and the Women's Environmental Network
www.wen.org.uk, which organises nappy activists' workshops.

Go M·A·D!

Organic

1

Detox with organic food

We often read that organic is better, but we often find out that it's costlier too. Is it worth the hassle?

The answer is a definite yes. In order to be registered organic, a farmer is allowed to use only seven natural pesticides – and even then only on a restricted basis. Conventional farms, however, can use as many as 450 registered pesticides, as well as fertilisers. The full health implications of this vast range of chemicals lingering around our food are still being studied, but it is now accepted that neurological disorders, a lowered sperm count, and certain cancers are caused by exposure to pesticides. Consider the following: the World Health Organisation estimates that 20,000 deaths are caused worldwide each year by pesticide exposure.

In addition, pesticides damage soil structure and destroy organisms living naturally within the soil. They also disrupt the food chain. Pesticide contamination of drinking water supplies in the UK costs £120 million annually.

It can be difficult for many of us to instantly shift our shopping patterns towards organic buying, but there are several initial steps you can take. To begin with, find out more about organic food from the Soil Association at www.soilassociation.co.uk, or call 01179 290661. For a comprehensive directory of all organic food suppliers, including shops, box schemes and restaurants go to the Soil Association's Organic Directory at www.soilassociation.org/SA/Directory.nsf. Two other important organisations that promote organic food are Sustain at www.sustain.org.uk (020 7837 1228) and the Henry Doubleday Research Association at www.hdra.org.uk (02476 303517) .

— 2 —
Choose one organic product to buy regularly

Deciding to always buy organic milk, or bread, for example, is a good way of getting into the routine of buying organic food. Then you can build up the range of organic products you buy as quickly as you like!

— 3 —
Look at the label

To make sure that food you believe to be organic really is, look for the European Certifying Authority code number. UK1 means the food has been certified by the government body UKROFS. UK5 means it has met the stricter requirements of the Soil Association, which certifies 70% of UK organic food. And just like other industries, the organic foods industry is rapidly going global – you could argue that buying organic food which has been transported from the other side of the world is doing little to help the environment. So look at the origin of the food too and try to buy local. Visit the Soil Association at www.soilassociation.org.uk, or call 01179 290661.

— 4 —
Drink organic too!

The alcoholic drinks industry is just as guilty of over-using pesticides as the food industry. Hops, for example, are sprayed 12–14 times a year with an average of 15 different pesticide products. The 'scorched earth' appearance of hop fields is intended to minimise weed growth, but it also minimises the diversity of wildlife species living in them. A great reason to drink organic is that, as it contains fewer additives, it might not give you such a bad hangover! There are several organic drinks companies, such as The Organic Spirits Company Ltd that sells organic gin and vodka. Visit www.junipergreen.org, or call 01483 894 650. Also try the Organic Wine Company at www.organicwinecompany.com, or call 01494 446 557.

'I'm not touching it if it's been sprayed!'

5

Join up to a box scheme

Box schemes or organic delivery companies save you the hassle of hunting for the organic produce you want. Check out Fresh Food Online at www.freshfood.co.uk (020 8969 0351), or the Organic Delivery company at www.organicdelivery.co.uk (020 7739 8181).

6

Buy organic cotton and wool

Cotton is the world's most sprayed crop, producing toxic run-off that contaminates nearby streams and rivers. And a lot of the non-organic cotton you buy is now also produced from Genetically Modified crops. The chemicals used in sheep-dips for non-organic wool production are toxic and leach into the water supply, as does the chlorine used for shrink-resistance treatments.

7

Free the countryside from pesticides!

The Organic Food and Farming Targets Bill Campaign is lobbying the government to pass a bill that will ensure 30% of land in England and Wales is organic by 2010. This is aiming high, but the possible effects would be dramatic, including the creation of 16,000 jobs, a 10% increase in the bird population, a 25% increase in the butterfly population and 11.5 million hectares of arable land no longer being sprayed with pesticides. The campaign is being driven by prominent organisations such as Sustain, Friends of the Earth, The Henry Doubleday Research Association and Pesticides Action Network-UK. Contact Sustain to find out how you can get involved. Visit www.sustainweb.org, or call 020 7837 1228.

—Packaging—

1

Unwrap!

Do you think twice when you buy a fish that is on a plastic tray, inside two separate plastic bags, that fit inside a cellophane-wrapped cardboard box? Or a bottle of mineral water made from five separate pieces of plastic? A staggering amount of packaging waste is produced in the UK each year – enough to fill 1.5 billion dustbins – most of which ends up in landfill sites where it can remain for hundreds of years. But why do we now have so much more packaging to throw away? Urbanisation and the increase in exotic consumer goods have lead to longer distances between producers and consumers, increasing the need for packaging to maintain freshness. And as households become smaller in size and lifestyles become more pressured, people buy more processed food and smaller portions, adding even more to the packaging mountain.

By buying local produce, and by giving the excess packaging back to the shop, we can cut down the amount of redundant packaging that goes through our own households. And there is plenty we can do with the waste itself.

2

Re-use aluminium foil

20,000 tonnes of aluminium foil packaging worth £8 million is wasted every year – equivalent to the weight of over 200 blue whales. Only 3,000 tonnes are recycled. Use a box with a lid or cover food bowls with plates instead of using cling film, which creates unnecessary waste.

3

Squash up your rubbish

If you are throwing away packaging squash it up, so that it takes up less room in the landfill.

'I hate the amount of packaging that food comes wrapped in these days.'

4

Avoid milk and juice cartons made from 'paper'

They are not made from paper alone. They are 75% paper, 20% polyethylene and 5% aluminium foil – a nightmare to recycle – and the majority are incinerated or put into a landfill site.

Buy refillables

Companies are now realising the wastefulness of buying the same product, such as washing up liquid, over and over again in a new bottle, when the old ones go straight to landfill sites. You can now buy cleaning products such as washing up liquid, dishwasher soap and floor cleaners in refillable bottles: find out more from Ecover at www.ecover.com (01635 528 240). For cosmetics and creams you can take part in the Body Shop refill scheme that gives you discounts on products when you take your bottle back to be refilled instead of buying a new one. Visit www.bodyshop.org.uk, or call 01903 731 500.

───────────── *6* ─────────────

Recycle steel cans

Every year we use 13 billion steel and aluminium cans which, placed end to end, would stretch to the moon...three times! It takes 350 times more energy to make cans from raw materials than it does from recycled material and if all the cans sold in the UK were recycled there would be 12 million fewer full dustbins each year. Three out of four cans on supermarket shelves are steel and therefore 100% recyclable.

───────────── *7* ─────────────

Say NO to bisphenol A

Find out if your supermarket uses packaging which contains bisphenol A. Bisphenol A is a hormone disrupter – a chemical that interferes with the body's hormones, hence disrupting the functioning of our day-to-day bodily functions. Some supermarkets are able to guarantee that their packaging, especially for baby food, is free from bisphenol A, but others aren't. It is only through pressure from their customers that they will take measures to stop its use. Find out more about hormone disrupters at www.foe.co.uk/campaigns/safer_chemicals.

Go M·A·D!

Paper

1

Cut down paper use, instead of trees

Despite our size, in the UK we still manage to be the world's fifth highest paper-users. Last year alone we managed to get through 12.9 million tonnes – over half of which was imported. Yet last year, we only recycled 38%. It's time to get that number up. Recycling really does make a difference, and isn't just about saving trees. Energy consumption and pollution savings can be huge: every tonne of recycled paper saves 32,000 litres of water and enough electricity to power an average house for six months. In addition, recycling creates three times more jobs than incineration.

So how can you make a difference? The first step is the easiest – simply get hold of a box for all your recycled paper at home. Several councils organise kerbside collection schemes that will pick up your waste paper from outside your front door once a week. If your council does not, keep writing to them until they do! Meanwhile, there are collection points for paper in civic amenity centres and supermarkets all over the UK. Go to www.recycle-more.co.uk or call the Recycling Helpline 0800 435576, which will connect you to your local council's recycling department.

2

KIDS – take old wallpaper to your school

Schools can use old wallpaper for painting on and for other activities in the classroom. They can also use old newspapers for covering tables in craft lessons or for making papier mâché.

3

Re-use paper!

A piece of paper which has been used once can be used again. And again. Make a notepad for telephone messages, reload your printer with paper which has been printed on one side when you are just printing for personal use, reuse envelopes and cut up old cards to make gift tags. Old newspapers can be put on the compost heap or used for animal bedding.

4

'One day son, all this will be junk mail!'

Eliminate junk mail!

100 million trees are used each year to make junk mail, 44% of which goes straight into the rubbish bin unread. This year you could receive around 400 pieces of junk mail. Unless, that is, you register with the Mailing Preference Service, Freepost 22, London W1E 7EZ (020 7766 4410). They will remove your name and address from the direct mail mailing lists.

Go M·A·D!

111

Recycle your Yellow Pages

If all the yellow pages used by Londoners were laid end to end they would stretch for 250 miles – further than the entire length of the River Thames. The yellow dye used for yellow pages means the paper cannot be recycled with your newspapers, but over half of local authorities now have schemes for recycling them. Nine out of ten authorities recycle other types of directory. Find out where your nearest directory recycling point is at www.directory-recycling.co.uk, or call 0800 783 1592.

Buy address labels from charities

Many charities sell labels which you can stick over the addresses on used envelopes so they can be used again – so you're saving paper and supporting a good cause at the same time. And when you buy envelopes, buy recycled. Recycled paper is manufactured with non-chlorine-based bleaching agents, and is free from optical brighteners, which are manufactured with petrochemicals and cause damage to flora and fauna when they leach into river water. Visit www.greenstat.co.uk, or call 01225 480556, or visit www.recycled-paper.co.uk, or call 01676 533 832.

Join the hemp movement

Hemp produces up to three or four times more pulp per acre than timber, and produces higher quality paper. There are no environmentally damaging bleaching processes in hemp paper production, and it recycles more times than wood pulp. It was one of the ancient world's most important crops, renowned for its properties in combating skin and respiratory diseases and used for fabrics and paper. Unlike other fibre crops, it does not need the intensive use of herbicides and pesticides to grow well, so is the perfect ecological crop for the 21st century. British farmers have been growing hemp commercially since 1993, but due to its connection with cannabis the government has been reluctant to support it. Give it your support, and the government's support will have to follow! You can buy hemp paper, but also products ranging from bags, to juggling balls, to frisbees, made from hemp at Mother Hemp www.shop.motherhemp.com, or call 07041 313233. Contact the Hemp Union at www.hemp-union.karoo.net/main.htm to find out more about the benefits of hemp, and for some recipe ideas.

-Pest control-

1

Most people associate pesticides with farming, yet 80% of our exposure to them comes from our homes and gardens

◆

Last year, UK householders doused their homes and gardens with 4,300 tonnes of pesticides, costing £35 million (and that's only counting the active ingredients, which account for 1–5% of the finished product). The figure is rising – sales of garden and home pesticides are increasing by 38% a year.

If you do use pesticides, keep yourself fully informed about their ingredients. Many people are completely unaware of the harmful content of the products they use (as the packets don't always explain their contents). To start to make a difference in your own pest control at home or in the garden, contact Pesticide Action Network UK, an excellent source of information, at www.pan-uk.org or call 020 7274 8895. There are invariably alternative, environmentally-friendly, methods of pest prevention and control.

2

If you get nits, avoid chemical head lice treatments

Chemicals used in head lice treatments can disrupt the immune system, cause burning sensations, skin irritation, hyperactivity and dizziness. Instead of using chemical treatments, thoroughly wash the hair with normal shampoo and conditioner, then wide-comb the hair to straighten it, then systematically fine-comb the hair from the roots to the tips to remove hatched lice.

3

Avoid using chemical insect sprays

One squirt of a chemical fly spray, and the toxic gases emitted will stay in the air for 72 hours. Chemicals such as dichlorvos and pyrethrins that are found in fly sprays also kill bees and aquatic life when their residues enter water systems. Perversely, they can also actually cause fly populations to increase, by strengthening their resistance to pesticides and killing species which are natural predators. 'Integrated pest management' is the general term given to controlling pests without resorting to chemicals, and involves altering the local environment to make it less attractive to pests. In the case of flies, this would involve cleaning out rubbish bins, disinfecting them and making sure there is no decaying food lying around. Natural fly deterrants include lemon, cloves, pine and cedar oils.
For natural methods of controlling other pests go to
www.symbios-witticism-page.com/bug.htm.

4

Use natural methods to control weeds

The damaging effects of pesticides are multiplied as they are washed by rainwater into sewers and then into waterways. Even weedkillers that claim to be safe such as Round-up or Path Clear have damaging effects. Roundup may be less toxic than some weedkillers but do you really want to be financing the promotion of Genetically Modified crops carried out by its manufacturer Monsanto? Also make sure you avoid any herbicide that contains Paraquat. Paraquat is so toxic that it is often used in suicide attempts and if it doesn't kill it causes permanent disability. Use organic alternatives. Phone 01932 253 666 for the Henry Doubleday Research Association's mail order catalogue.

5

Use non-toxic methods of snail and slug control

Chemical slug treatments do not degrade, so their toxins remain in the environment indefinitely. And as slugs are the hedgehog's favourite food, you will be indirectly poisoning hedgehogs too. There are several alternative methods of slug control such as inter-planting herbs – slugs don't like spiky, aromatic plants. Spreading ash or broken eggshells on the earth also works wonders in deterring them.

6

Dispose of pesticides safely

Find out from your local council about their chemical waste-disposal schemes. Whether pesticides are put down the drain or dumped in landfill sites, they make their way into our drinking water. The purification process then uses millions of litres of water and the cost of the energy needed is added to YOUR water bill.

7

Say no to lindane!

Thankfully, after persistent campaigning by environmental groups, in December 2000 the European Commission ratified a ban on the use of lindane in agriculture and gardening. Lindane is an organochlorine pesticide. It is a possible human carcinogen, an endocrine disrupter and is highly volatile, which means it enters the atmosphere and is later deposited in rain. Cases of human poisoning by lindane have been reported. Unfortuneately, lindane is still used in the southern hemisphere, particularly on cocoa plantations producing chocolate that is transported all over the world. Organisations such as the Pesticide Action Network UK, the Soil Association and Women's Environmental Network (www.gn.apc.org/wen, tel: 020 7481 9004) have formed the Ban Lindane Campaign and are now working on the next stages of the ban. Find out about it at www.pan-uk.org/banlindane.

Pets

1

Pets are consumers too

◆

Thanks to great work by the RSPCA over the years, and to the fact that the UK is a nation of animal-lovers, pets now have it much better in this country than they do in many others. Almost half the households in the UK own a pet, and they are often used for therapy in nursing homes and for alleviating clinical depression.

Whilst pets and pet-owners might be better off today – is the environment? Cats, for example, are notorious killers of wild animals. A survey in 1997 estimated that the UK's 7.5 million pet cats could be killing at least 300 million animals and birds every year – whereas a simple bell round your cat's neck could help to reduce that number significantly.

The pet pampering industry can have environmental repercussions too. Your pets are just as happy chewing and scratching on home-made toys as they are on resource-depleting, environment-damaging plastic. With a little care and attention, your pet can be your best friend – and the environment's, too.

Scoop that poop!

The British canine population is around 6.8 million, producing 900 tonnes of excrement a day (that's the equivalent of 15 million sausages!). Dog excretement can contain the minute eggs of roundworm, which are then washed into the soil where they live for up to two years. If they then enter the human body they can hatch, producing larvae that burrow through the gut and wander around the body, damaging the liver, lungs and eyes and sometimes leading to blindness. Children playing in parks are the most at risk, so bag it, and bin it!

— 3 —

Buy dry pet food instead of the canned variety

The UK spends £600 billion a year on canned pet food. Tins can be recycled but their production and transportation requires energy and effort that is greatly reduced when you buy dry food in bulk.

Find out about organic and vegetarian options from Bluepet at www.bluepet.co.uk, or call 024 7639 6961.

— 4 —

Buy pets from rescue centres instead of pet shops

Every year, the RSPCA takes 280,000 creatures into its hospitals and clinics, and in 2000 Battersea Dogs' Home took in 10,869 dogs and 4,140 cats. The numbers are rising and there are always dogs and cats waiting for someone to offer them a good home. Instead of encouraging the breeding of yet more pets, why don't you give homes to those already in need? Visit www.dogshome.org, or call 020 7622 3626, and www.rspca.org.uk, or call 0870 0101181.

Don't use commercial flea sprays or collars

Most of them contain organophosphates and carbamates, such as carbaryl, that work by attacking pests' nervous systems, but these chemicals have been known to cause reproductive problems and abnormal behaviour. Use a non-toxic flea collar or try adding garlic pills and brewer's yeast to pets' food (these products can be bought in pet supply stores).

6

Have your cat neutered!

One female un-neutered cat can be responsible for 50 million offspring and descendants if it has two litters each of six kittens. The surging cat population means that thousands are abandoned each year – in 1999 the RSPCA re-homed 46,786 cats and had many more on waiting lists.

7

Stamp out pet trade cruelty

Did you know that puppies bred intensively throughout the world to be sold in UK pet shops are often kept in dark, cold and cramped conditions, and are looked after by people more concerned with making money than the welfare of the animals? Indiscriminate breeding increases the risk of genetic and behavioural problems in the litters and the puppies are often separated from their mother at a very early age. Help the National Canine Defence League campaign against puppy farming. Visit www.ncdl.org.uk, or call 020 7837 0006.

A single shipload of green iguana can contain 2,000–5,000 creatures, carrying them thousands of miles, often illegally, from their native habitat to an unnatural one in captivity, and allowing their natural population to decline. Iguanas are the most commonly traded exotic reptile in the UK, but Britain imports a total of over one million live reptiles and amphibians a year, including boas, pythons, chameleons and geckos. It's not only reptiles, but also birds, fish and mammals who are swept up in this trade. Find out more, and how you can help stop it, at www.traffic.org or by calling Traffic International on 01223 277 427.

Plastic

1

Plastic's drastic

Plastic is manufactured from crude oil, and is designed to resist decay – that's why it's used in food packaging – and that's also why it is an ecological nightmare. Where does it all end up? In a recent survey of the Bristol Channel coastline, a staggering 550 plastic bottles per kilometre were found.

But the problem is a truly global one. On the Mediterranean seabed, half a kilometre down, plastic bags accumulate at a density of up to 80 per hectare. Cattle develop ulcerated bellies and eventually die after swallowing plastic bags. Their bodies will slowly decompose, but the plastic bags remain.

The mixture of different plastics used in products means that recycling them is difficult (at the moment only 11% of plastic is recycled in the UK), so most plastic is used once then spends thousands of years polluting the environment.

The first difference you can make is simple.
REDUCE your USE!

KIDS – make deodorant bottle paint-pens

Roll-on deodorant bottles with removable balls make ideal painting pens for kids. Fill them with non-toxic paint. You can also use plastic bottles to make funnels by cutting the bottom with a sharp knife. If you need a fine filter, stretch a piece of clean muslin over the neck.

— 3 —

Always SNUB –
Say No to Unwanted Bags

UK shoppers use eight billion plastic carrier bags a year (that's 134 per person). Consolidate all your shopping in one bag rather than getting a new one at each shop. For the truly committed, take your own shopping bag with you.

'Want a plastic bag for those things?'

— 4 —

If you have to buy a drink in a plastic bottle DON'T THROW IT AWAY!

Re-use it, and then take it to your nearest recycling plant. In the UK we buy 15 million plastic bottles a day. Only 3% of those are recycled despite the fact that most bottles are now made of PET, an easily recyclable plastic – recycling just one plastic bottle can save the energy needed to power a 60-watt lightbulb for 6 hours. Look for the number 1 inside a triangle on the bottom of the bottle – the US 1–7 grading system now appears on most plastic packaging, and 1 is the symbol for PET. In Germany 70% of PET bottles are now recycled. Find your nearest plastic recycling plant at www.wastepoint.co.uk/wasteconnect or by calling 0800 435576.

Go M·A·D!

Never use plastic in microwaves and avoid using it in fridges

Heat and cold speed up the process of plastic degradation, accelerating the movement of plastic molecules into food. Who wants to eat plastic for dinner?

Avoid products containing PVC

Since the 1960s scientists have known that the softening agent phthalates (pronounced 'thal-lates') leak out of PVC. The most commonly used phthalate, DEHP, is listed as a possible human carcinogen and causes liver, kidney and reproductive damage. Greenpeace has a list of all the products we use that contain PVC at www.greenpeace.org. They range from tupperware containers to garden furniture and window frames.

If your council doesn't have a plastic recycling facility, set up a petition and keep hassling them until they do

Recycling plastic is expensive because of the hundreds of different types of plastic used. A crisp packet can contain three layers of different plastics. At the moment, we only recycle 15% of our plastic packaging. But if some councils manage it there is no reason why others can't – and they only will when they realise it's something you the voters care about! A pioneering recycling unit called Reclaim was set up in Sheffield in 1989, providing employment for people with mental health illnesses, and now recycles 100 tonnes of plastic film a year and 350 tonnes of plastic bottles. Write to both your local council and local MP. Find out about recycling plastics and how to go about setting up schemes in your areas from RECOUP. Visit www.recoup.org, or call 01684 272185.

Go M·A·D!

Presents

1

Be a Green giver

Sometimes it seems as if the year is one long gift-buying spree - with Christmas, Easter, Mothers' Day, Fathers' Day, Valentines, leaving parties, something to bring back for the folks from holiday, not to mention birthdays!

And what might the present be? Something bought hurriedly at lunch-time which does the job, yet which was made in China, transported to the US, then distributed to a UK warehouse before making its way to a local shop, burning up thousands of miles of transport fuel in the process?

Then there's the wrapping paper, the gift tags, and the little ribbon bows on top, all ending up in someone's dustbin the next day.
We spend so much money on the many presents we give, and use up so much of the world's resources in the process.

With a little planning, we can find a way of giving presents which are thoughtful, original, and a real pleasure to receive. And which make a positive difference to the environment, as well.

KIDS – next time it's a friend's birthday make them a card

Modern art is often a case of personal taste! Haven't you looked at a picture and wondered how it ever became famous? Experiment with your own artistic talent using old cards, coloured paper, foil, string and other nic-nacs that are lying around.

— 3 —

Give a recycled present

This doesn't have to mean a reject from your great aunt! Glass tableware, furniture made from driftwood... there's no end of original recycled presents once you look around. Wastewatch is full of good ideas and details of where you can find original recycled gifts. Go to www.wastewatch.org.uk or phone the Waste Watch Wasteline on 0870 243 0136. Don't forget charities also run year-round mail order services and are a good source of recycled present ideas.

AND MAKE SURE YOU LOOK AFTER IT!

— 4 —

Give a present of your time

Why not arrange for yourself and your friend to go on a trip to the theatre, a concert, the cinema or a sporting event? No wrapping involved, yet it's far more personal than a book or record token!

Go M.A.D!

5

Don't give mass-produced flowers

The beautiful bunch of roses you buy in a florists or supermarket has probably been grown in a greenhouse the other side of the world at a huge environmental and social cost. In Colombia, with a flower industry worth $600 million, two-thirds of flower workers suffer from illnesses caused by pesticide exposure. One-fifth of the chemicals used there are carcinogens or toxins, the use of which is restricted in the US! And while you may pay £2 for four carnations in a shop, that is more than a flower worker earns in a day, after picking 400 of them. The treasured Lake Naivasha in Kenya is rapidly being drained into the surrounding flower farms and polluted with pesticides. How about growing your own flowers instead? Or give a plant, that will live for much longer than cut flowers.

6

Give a Squirrel!

Well, not exactly. But through wildlife charities you can organise for a rare squirrel, seal, puffin or owl to be adopted as a present. The money you spend on the present (often as little as £15) goes towards the organisation's work to protect that endangered species. Two organisations that do this are the Wildlife Trusts – visit www.wildlifetrusts.org.uk, or call 01636 677 711 – and the Barn Owl Trust (visit www.barnowltrust.org.uk, or call 01364 653 026.)

7

Give to Make A Difference

Make a present of a year's membership of an environmental organisation. Environmental organisations rely on their membership to be able to do the work they do. Hunt around for a small organisation that has a specific relevance for the person receiving the present. There are thousands of small organisations ranging from the British Beekeepers Association or the British Hedgehog Preservation Society to the British Cave Research Association. F or a list of all of them and website links go to www.ethicaljunction.org, or call 0161 236 3637.

Go M·A·D!

Reading

1

Transform your world with words!

◆

Books help us make sense of life. In a world where immediacy rules, where TV presents us with information at such a speed that we do not have the time to think about it before it is replaced by another image, thought or story, reading hands you back control over the pace and direction of your thinking. Considering the media is owned and controlled by the same companies it is supposed to be scrutinising, do you think it always gives the whole truth? As in any other industry, ethics and morals are often pushed aside by financial interests - which is all the more dangerous when that industry is supposed to be supplying people with reliable information. Books can help you make up your own mind.

The Barefoot Book of Heroic Children

Read the stories of Anne Frank, Sundiata and other children whose courage and response to situations that they felt needed changing show us that, in a world of adult-made decisions and disasters, children can, and often do, make a difference. *The Barefoot Book of Heroic Children* is by Rebecca Hazell. Published by Barefoot Books. ISBN 1 902283 22 8. £14.99

The Great Food Gamble

This eye-opening read gets to the roots of modern farming practices, such as factory-farming and extensive transportation, and unearths some ugly truths. It examines the true costs of the intensive use of pesticides and antibiotics in agriculture to the environment and to our health. But most importantly, it poses the serious questions of whether, and how, we can reverse this trend, by returning to localised production. *The Great Food Gamble* is by John Humphrys. Published by Hodder and Stoughton General. ISBN 0340 770 457. £12.99

Stormy Weather – 101 solutions to climate change

Speaking confidently of the need for action this book lays out the problems facing the earth, and then presents us with 101 case studies of responses that are actually working. *Stormy Weather* is by Guy Dauncey and Patrick Mazza and is published by New Society Publishers Ltd. ISBN 0865714215. £14.99

5

Ancient Futures, Learning from Ladakh

Ladakh, or 'little Tibet' is a desert land in the Western Himalayas. This is the story of its forced entry into the modern world, its consequent near-breakdown and renewal against the odds. It has been translated into more than 30 languages, and has led to grassroots counter-development movements in every corner of the globe, from Devon to Mongolia. *Ancient Futures* is by Helena Norberg-Hodge and published by Rider. ISBN 0712606564. £9.99

6

The Case Against the Global Economy

This is a revealing collection that brings together leading economic, agricultural and environmental experts who argue that globalisation and free trade produce exactly the opposite effects to what they promised. If this doesn't make you want to resist economic globalisation, then nothing will. *The Case Against the Global Economy* is edited by Edward Goldsmith and Jerry Mander and is published by Earthscan. ISBN 1853837423. £14.95

7

Set up a book club – turn words into actions

A book does not end when you close the last page. Book clubs are springing up all over the country as people rediscover the pleasure and benefits of sharing the books they read. How about setting up an ecological book club? At each meeting you could discuss one of the major environmental issues, such as climate change, agriculture or globalisation, choosing a few relevant books to read beforehand. Publishers which specialise in environmental books and will help you with more ideas include Green Books www.greenbooks.co.uk (01803 863843), Earthscan www.earthscan.co.uk (020 7837 1816) and you could also try the Schumacher book service www.schumacher.org.uk (0117 903 1081).

For comprehensive information and case studies to supplement your meetings try the One World website www.oneworld.net which examines the stories behind mainstream news.

Sewage and water pollution

1

Think before you flush

Every time you flush your lavatory, the contents disappear – only to resurface somewhere else! It's not a pleasant thought, of course, and after all, we do have a sewage system to deal with it, don't we? Well, it depends what you flush – apart from the obvious! We flush an extraordinary range of chemicals and loose items from cigarette butts to cotton buds. British swimmers can still contract illnesses from gastroenteritis to hepatitis A. In fact people who spend a lot of time in the sea, such as surfers, are three times more likely to contract hepatitis A than the rest of the public.

It's not only people who are at risk – chemicals and washing products that find their way into our river systems kill plants, aquatic life, and even land animals who drink from rivers. Toilet flushing accounts for the largest proportion of water-use in the UK – 35% of our domestic water goes down the lavatory. Awareness of where your used water goes is the first step towards transforming the quality of water in our rivers and around our coasts.

2

Don't flush it, bin it!

Three-quarters of blockages in water pipes are due to disposables such as sanitary towels, razor blades, syringes, even ladies' tights and cotton buds – over 75% of toilet debris on beaches last year was composed of the plastic sticks from cotton buds! So don't do it! Birds mistake tampon applicators for food and often choke on them.

3

Never use optical brighteners to wash your clothes

Packets which claim they wash 'brighter than bright' or 'whiter than white', usually contain optical brighteners that disrupt the ecosystems in rivers because they cannot be broken down. Several washing detergents also contain phosphates, causing algal blooms that deprive river life of oxygen and disrupt treatment processes. Use natural plant-based washing products that don't contain phosphates. Visit www.ecover.com, or call 01635 528240 to find out about Ecover's products, or for Eco-Co, visit www.ecozone.com, or call 020 8777 3121.

4

Don't use bleach to clean the lavatory

Bleach may do a good job of killing the bacteria in the toilet, but it also contains caustic soda that kills the bacteria which digest the sewage at the sewage plant, making it difficult and expensive to treat properly. You can buy ecological loo cleaners from Eco-Co Products (www.ecozone.com, or call 020 8777 3121) or the Green Shop (www.greenshop.co.uk, or call 01452 770 629).

Go M·A·D!

5

Filter your own water

The ageing infrastructure of water pipes and some of the cleaning processes used for water mean that, by the time it reaches you, it is far more than pure and simple H_2O! Tap water can contain chlorine, ammonia, bacteria, dissolved organic matter, suspended solids such as rust and dirt, and heavy metals such as aluminium, copper and lead. These can easily be removed with simple water filtration methods. Find out about them at www.freshwaterfilter.com or call Fresh Water Filter on 020 8597 3223 or the Pure H_2O company at www.pureh2O.co.uk, tel: 01784 221 188.

6

Report incidents of water pollution to the Environment Agency

Don't assume that someone else has reported it already. Even if they have, if the pollution is still there clearly no action has been taken and they need reminding! If you see a foamy scum or brown slick on the surface of rivers, lakes or the sea, or smell sewage, get on the phone to the Environment Agency's hotline on 0800 80 70 60.

7

Campaign for cleaner water!

By 2005, less than a quarter of the UK's sewage will receive full tertiary (ultraviolet radiation) treatment. Most of the rest only receives primary treatment. Primary treated sewage contains 10% of the faecal particles in raw sewage, secondary has 1% and tertiary has only 0.0035%. When sewage is not treated properly it prevents the use of water for irrigation, fisheries, recreation, and of course, drinking. Phone your water company or contact the Environment Agency online at www.environment-agency.gov.uk or by phone on 0800 80 70 60 and ask if your area is receiving full treatment – if not, write to them demanding to know why and reminding them that full treatment does not have to work out more expensive than secondary treatment in the long run. Help campaigning group Surfers Against Sewage lobby for full treatment of sewage throughout the UK, and find out all about sewage and water pollution at www.sas.org.uk or call 01872 553 001.

Shopping

1

Be an ethical consumer

◆

Global warming, species extinction, animal testing, the arms trade, and human rights abuses... all of these things can seem way beyond our control. But as a consumer you DO have control, because many of these problems are either caused or perpetuated by corporations funded by the money which you spend on their products.

Every purchase you make has either a direct or indirect effect on the environment. When you exercise your power by choosing where and what to buy, and where and what NOT to buy, you help change the world for the better.

The first step to becoming a better shopper is to find out the stories behind the shelves. Here are some excellent places to start buying your way to a better planet: Ethical Consumer www.ethicalconsumer.org (0161 226 29290), Ethical Junction www.ethical-junction.org (0161 236 3637), Get Ethical www.getethical.com (020 7419 7258). You can find all the background to ethical consumerism at One World's site: www.oneworld.org.

Buy nothing on Buy Nothing Day!

A simple but effective way of having a break from consumerism and reminding ourselves how easy it is to become caught up in the 'shop till you drop' culture. Find out more at www.buynothingday.co.uk or visit the Canadian 'subvertising' site www.adbusters.org/campaigns/bnd. Another step you can try all year round is to make a list of everything you buy during the week. You may realise how little of it you really need.

Avoid shopping in supermarkets whenever possible

In the UK, 60–70% of the food we buy comes from one of the four largest supermarket companies (Tesco, Sainsbury's, Safeway and Asda). This concentration of control means farmers are forced to accept low prices for their produce and also that food is sourced from developing countries where supermarkets can be sure of cheap labour and non-existent pollution laws. And while global warming is the greatest threat to life on earth, transport pollution is the largest single cause of global warming, and the average item you buy in a supermarket has travelled 1,000 miles. Supermarkets act as giant vacuum cleaners, sucking money out of an area and putting it in the banks of distant shareholders. Hundreds of jobs are lost each time one opens up. And this is only the tip of the iceberg...

Buy recycled!

If there was no market for recycled goods, recycling would not occur. And it's not as hard as you may think to find recycled products – the National Recycling Forum has a database of limitless recycled products and where you can find them, visit www.nrf.org.uk, or call 020 7089 2100. Look for the möbius loop symbol which means that a product has been recycled. And remember, re-using is a form of recycling. Charity shops and jumble sales are full of second-hand goods with years of use still in them.

Use farmers' markets

Farmers' markets, springing up at a rate of two a week throughout the UK, keep money within the local economy. At a Bristol market farmers estimated they could make £30 more per lamb than if they sold it to a supermarket, even while selling it to the customer at a cheaper than supermarket price. All products are grown, reared, caught, brewed, pickled, baked, smoked or processed by the stallholder – for once you will actually know where your food has come from. And because they are local they cut down on transport, packaging and pollution. Visit www.farmersmarkets.net, or call 01225 787 914.

Buy locally

Just think of the resources wasted and the pollution created by shifting goods all over the world – and increasingly by air. In 1999, 44,000 tonnes of live animals and meat was imported from Argentina to the EU, 40,000 tonnes from Poland and 70,000 tonnes from Brazil: in the same year 874,211 tonnes were exported from Europe. If you buy all your goods from local suppliers it creates a demand that stimulates the local economy, rejuvenates the community, and moves towards a goal of sustainability.

Wrest the power from the multinationals!

Choose two multinational corporations (MNCs) with harmful environmental policies and boycott their products. You may be surprised at just how many different products they sell. Consumers have the collective power to change companies' policies and therefore their effect on the environment. Success stories range from the campaign by Save the Children and trades unions that led to sports companies phasing out child labour for football stitching within 18 months of the campaign's launch, to the hugely successful awareness campaign in Europe against GM foods .

Visit www.ethicalconsumer.org for more success stories or contact Corporate Watch at www.corporatewatch.co.uk (01865 791 391), or go to the Beyond McDonald's website www.mcspotlight.org/beyond.

Sleeping

1

On average, you'll spend the best part of 25 years of your life asleep

◆

That's a long, long time when there's little you can do to help the environment. Or is it? Twenty-five years of leaving the heating on, or a comforting night-light, is one mighty use of resources. What about that hot shower that'll be waiting for you in the morning? A timer switch means you can set the boiler to heat your water for when you need it, rather than through the night.

But above all, a good night's sleep can sharpen the mind, preparing you for the day ahead. Sometimes it can be easy to make a difference – sometimes it takes mental energy.

Get a good night's sleep, and you can make a difference in everything you do.

KIDS – make a mobile hanging toy

From scrap materials of course! This is not only a good way to re-use scraps, but mobiles are a perfect way of lulling a baby or child to sleep. Coathangers are good to use as a starting point.

3

Send your appliances to sleep at the same time as you

In the UK we spend £200 million a year on the energy used when appliances are on standby. Before you go to bed unplug computers, VCRs, TVs and stereo systems.

4

Sleep in organic cotton pyjamas and bedclothes

Organic cotton has been grown without the use of pesticides and is unbleached, so does not involve the emission of toxic formaldehyde in its production process. Places where you can buy organic cotton include: Green Fibres Eco Goods and Garments (www.greenfibres.com, or call 01803 868 001), Gossypium.co.uk (www.gossypium.co.uk, or call 01273 897 509) and The Healthy House (www.healthy-house.co.uk, or call 01453 752 216).

5

During winter, wrap up warm in bed instead of having the heating on full all night

The average household spends £400 on energy bills during winter. Just by turning down the heating 1°C or using the heating for one hour less each day you can cut your fuel bill by 10%.

Sleep cosy on a natural fibre mattress

Mattresses made from cotton filling, coconut fibre or horsehair have properties which synthetic materials can never match. They are good conductors of body moisture, whereas if you sleep on synthetic mattresses you find your moisture collects in pools on the surface. And they don't sag in the middle, so save the NHS a fortune in mending bad backs.

'Now I lay me down to sleep,
I pray the Lord my soul to keep,
Lord, save the world from going to pot,
Just let me keep my heater hot.'

7

Make sure you get a good night's sleep!

Peace of body means peace of mind. Drink decaffeinated tea or coffee in the evening and cut down on nicotine. Alcohol can also disrupt sleep. Chemicals that are found in chocolate, Chianti wine and cheddar cheese can trigger heart palpitations during the night. A light snack before you go to bed can promote sleep, but a big meal forces your digestive system to work overtime, keeping you awake. And using your mobile phone in bed will also disrupt your sleep: electromagnetic fields from the phone increase brain activity during the early phase of sleep.

Go M·A·D!

─Technology─

─ 1 ─

We can now link up across the planet, let's try and link WITH the planet.

Whoever predicted that the world would only ever need five big computers is probably swallowing their words! They're all around us, and we're upgrading and replacing them all the time. But it takes a lot of natural resources to make a computer. Seven litres of crude oil are used to make the plastic inside just one system. Old computers can cause problems too. Hazardous computer waste includes lead, and the nickel and cadmium in the batteries used in laptop computers.

Mobile phones have become an extraordinary growth phenomenon, too. Within a few years there will be 1.3 billion people using mobile phones globally, before we've fully understood their effects on our health. What we do know is that mobiles are by far the most radioactive domestic appliances ever invented, with a power density twenty times more powerful than users' exposure to microwave ovens.

Computers and mobile communications have promised, and provided, an incredible technological revolution. But while they have become a part of life, they have also become another environmental problem.

'Oh God, look Bert – a pretty little upstart in the office. We're for the scrap heap, I just know it!'

2

KIDS – cut down on mobile phone use

Around a quarter of mobile phone users are under 18. Children are more at risk from phone radiation because their thinner skulls mean it penetrates the brain more easily, degrading their developing immune systems and nervous systems. Yet the government still allows the phone companies to market their products to children.

3

Screensavers don't save energy

In fact sometimes they use more energy than when the computer is in use. If you are going to be away from your computer for over an hour, switch it to sleep mode or turn it off. A computer monitor left on overnight wastes enough energy to laser print 800 A4 pages.

4

When you use your mobile phone indoors make sure you are near a window

Radiation from mobile phone signals can change the chemistry of the blood/brain barrier, which normally allows certain chemicals across and not others. Signal strengths can be up to ten times greater by a window, so the handset uses less power to establish contact with the mast. Make sure you have the handset near the window side too, so that less of the signal passes through your head.

5

Recycle your computers and phones

Globally, over 31 million PCs are thrown away ever year. For every three new computers now built, two old computers become obsolete, and in the UK three out of four computers 'disappear' after just one owner. But there are several organisations which recycle computers either for resale or for re-use by schools and charities, such as Computers for Charity (www.computersforcharity.org.uk or 01288 361 177), and Community Computers (www.community-computers.co.uk or 0113 293 0168). You can also donate old computers to Computer Aid International (www.computeraid.org or 020 7281 0091) which has so far sent over 4,000 computers to schools and community groups in Africa, Latin America and the Caribbean. And don't throw away your phone either! It's estimated that there are 20 million potentially toxic redundant mobile phones in the UK. Environmental Mobile Control will collect your phone for free and recycle it.
Visit www.emc-recycle.com or call 01283 516 259.

6

Look for the Energy Star symbol when buying computer appliances

The Energy Star is a US rating system that also applies to goods sold in the UK. When you buy a printer, modem, scanner or monitor with the Energy Star sign you know it will be one of the most efficient models. If you use Energy Star computer equipment you could save up to £25 over per year per computer. Find out more about Energy Star products at www.energystar.gov.

7

Say NO to phone mastheads by schools

For people living close to mobile phone masts there is nowhere to hide from the 'electrosmog' they create. There is evidence that long-term exposure to this radiation can cause serious illnesses such as leukaemia and lymphoma in certain exposed people, and much anecdotal evidence linking it with headaches, sleep disruption and impairment of short-term memory. No-one, but especially children and the elderly, should be exposed to these risks. To find out about phone mast issues and support the campaign against them, visit www.mastaction.org or write to Mast Action UK, MAUK Head Office, PO Box 312, Hertfordshire EN7 5ZE.

Time Out

1

Give yourself a break – and the environment!

◆

Leisure is one of the fastest growing industries in the UK, accounting for over 10% of total employment and over 25% of total consumer expenditure. But a lot of this money goes towards quick-fix enjoyment that gives little thought to its long-term impact on the environment.

If we fill our free time with more products and clutter, our time off can be just as hectic as our time on! A weekend may only be two days long but if you use it well, it can become a mini-holiday. And if you spend a lot of your working life taking from the environment, how about using some of your spare time to give something back, to brush the sand back over your ecological footprint?

BREAK GLASS
IN CASE OF
STRESS

KIDS – have a TV-free week

Children aged 6 to 16 in the UK spend on average three hours a day watching TV, compared with the European average of two hours. We don't compare that well with children from other countries when it comes to other activities, either: 54% of UK children read books in their free time compared to 91% of children in The Netherlands; in the UK, 33% of children read newspapers compared with 89% in Sweden. A TV-free week would create 21 hours to fill with sport, reading, exploring your local area, meeting up with friends, being outdoors....You might find you don't miss it too much!

—————————— 3 ——————————

Like taking photos? Use 36-exposure camera films instead of 24

This reduces waste from packaging and processing chemicals by a third, and can save 30% in cost.

—————————— 4 ——————————

Go Barefoot

Your feet absorb 3 times your body weight with each step and contain thousands of nerve endings connected to different parts of the body – no wonder they like to breathe. By going barefoot you are effectively giving yourself a gentle foot massage and keeping the rest of your body happy.

Boycott greyhound racing

Greyhound racing is a ruthless multi-million pound industry. Of the 30,000 greyhounds that are bred for racing each year, 10,000 are killed before their first race, and a further 12,000 will be injured during a race. A greyhound's potential lifespan is 14 years, but they are often killed when their peak racing time is over, at the age of two or three. Find out more from Greyhound Rescue at www.greyhoundrescue.co.uk or by calling 020 7188 1068.

Go somewhere wild this weekend

The more people show they appreciate Britain's fast disappearing wild places, the more they will be guaranteed protection. Contact the Federation of City Farms and Community Gardens to find your nearest city farm www.farmgarden.org.uk (0117 923 1800). Friends of the Earth will tell you where your nearest 'wild place' is www.foe.co.uk/wildplaces or call 020 7490 1555. Or if you fancy some duck-spotting go to a wetland centre - contact the Wildfowl and Wetlands Trust www.wwt.org.uk (01453 891900). British Waterways conserves 2000 miles of canals and inland rivers. To find out more go to www.britishwaterways.co.uk or call 01923 226 422.

Bring fair trade to the coffee trade

Coffee is the world's second largest export after oil. But its producers don't reap the benefits. Millions of coffee growers in South and Central America, Asia and Africa have watched helplessly as the prices for their product have fallen by 50% in the past two years. Meanwhile we're happy to pay £2 or over for a coffee in a high street store – 14 times the price of raw coffee at the point of export. A successful campaign by Global Exchange meant that in October 2000, 2,300 Starbucks stores introduced a fair trade coffee bean onto their menu. Now they are campaigning for the chain to make Fair Trade coffee the coffee of the day all year round. Find out more at www.globalexchange.org. And every time you go out for coffee, ask for Fair Trade.

Toys

1

Play for the planet

In Britain, we go mad on toys. Christmas, unsurprisingly, is the key buying time, with 55% of all toy sales taking place in the final quarter of the year. Boys under 14 on average have £154 spent on them per year, and girls, £142.

In addition, according to the British Association of Toy Retailers, children are getting older younger, too – that means they grow out of their toys earlier, and want new ones.

All of which comes to a staggering £1.67 billion spent on toys in the UK every year. That's an awful lot of plastic – in every sense!

So many toys can do so much damage. Often made on the other side of the world by children who receive next to nothing for their labour. They are transported from country to country, burning up fuel, and wrapped in packaging that contributes to global waste. And how often have you given a brand new toy to a young child, only to find them playing with the cardboard box it came in! Why not make a difference in the toys you give – it can be great fun for you as well as the children!

— 2 —

Make your own!

Colourful old clothes can be perfect to make stuffed toys, beanbag toys or rag dolls. And some will have a whole new lease of life in a fancy dress box.

— 3 —

Take used toys to charity shops, doctors' surgeries or hospitals

If your child has grown out of a toy, there will still be a child who can get hours of fun from it. If you're a toy hoarder, do you really think your grandchildren will want to play with toys that were all the rage 30 years ago? Better for someone else to get use out of them now.

— 4 —

Play safe

All toys sold in the UK should have the European – CE – safety mark – if they don't, steer clear. The 'lion' mark, a triangle with a lion inside it, tells you that the toy is made by a member of the British Toy and Hobby Association – Visit www.btha.co.uk, or call 020 7701 7271 – and is an extra guarantee that it will be safe. Other simple steps you can take when buying toys are to check for sharp edges or corners (children have inquisitive fingers!) and for choking hazards such as loose hair or eyes on a teddy bear.

— 5 —

Only buy rechargeable, solar or non-toxic batteries

Most batteries contain toxic metals such as cadmium, mercury and nickel that leak into the environment when they are thrown away. Teach your child how to recharge their batteries – get them into good habits! When you do buy batteries choose alkaline manganese batteries which are free from toxic heavy metals. And how about buying a solar-powered battery charger? You can find them at www.getethical.com.

Never buy toys containing PVC

Plastics, especially PVC, can contain phthalates (pronounced 'thal-lates'), that are harmful chemicals found in many plastic-based products, and are suspected of disrupting the development of the testicles, reducing sperm counts, and damaging the liver and kidneys. Nine European countries have banned certain phthalates from teething objects and toys for young children, but those imported from some Asian countries contain up to 55% phthalates by weight.

'PVC free? Sure they are... honest!'

Bring fairness to the toy industry! Buy fair trade toys

Children working on assembly lines in Haiti in 1996 were paid eight pence an hour to churn out Pocahontas and Mickey Mouse pyjamas for Disney. All over the developing world, children are employed to make toys for your children to play with. Fair Trade shops sell toys which ensure their manufacturers get a fair price for what they do and that their employment meets strict ethical standards. Find out more from Traidcraft at www.traidcraft.co.uk (0191 491 0591) or from the British Association of Fair Trade Shops on 01189 569361.

Go M·A·D!

Travel

1

Leave your destination as you found it

Tourism is now the world's largest industry. By 2010, there'll be one billion of us flying round the world each year, using resources, adding to pollution and affecting the environment around us as we go.

However if a billion people will be travelling by then, five billion won't. Just five nations (US, Japan, Germany, UK and France) account for over half of all the world's tourist spending. That means that many people are hosts to tourists, without actually travelling themselves.

It's worth considering that the consumption of resources you are used to may be enormous compared with that of the people whose country you are visiting. For example, an average golf course in a tropical country such as Thailand uses 1,500kg of chemical fertilisers, pesticides and herbicides per year and gets through as much water as 60,000 rural villages.

But this isn't about putting a dampener on our holidays. The year 2002 has been designated the International Year of Sustainable Tourism – there are so many ways of having a brilliant holiday and reducing our environmental impact.

Read up about your destination

Tourism comes from the Hebrew word 'Tora', which means to study, learn or search. Much modern tourism has come a long way from these origins but by knowing about a country before you visit the mark you leave is more likely to be a positive one. Try to learn at least five words of the language before you go, too, and keep learning while you're there. As well as having your own good memories hopefully the people you meet will also have good memories of you.

— 3 —

Use small, location-specific travel operators rather than the giant travel agencies

80% of British package holidays are booked through Thompsons, Airtours, First Choice and Thomas Cook. These companies tend to undercut prices, use imported goods rather than supporting the local economy and can switch the destination of package tours with little warning, thereby destroying the livelihood of local hotel owners and tour operators.

— 4 —

For short journeys, try to avoid air travel

Over short distances (less than 500km) air travel produces around three times more CO_2 per passenger than rail. Aviation generates nearly as much CO_2 annually as that from all human activities in Africa. One long-haul return flight can produce more CO_2 per passenger than the average UK motorist in one year. Scientists have predicted that by 2015, half of the annual destruction of the ozone layer will be caused by air travel. And if you are flying from Luton airport, make sure your pay your 'Green Tax'. The 0.2p per mile tax helps fund a local tree planting programme. Encourage other airports to adopt a 'Green Tax'.

5

Use public transport, hire a bike or walk where convenient

This is a good way of meeting local people and getting to know the local area other than through the windows of a tour bus.

6

Leave nature alone

The trade in endangered species – and that includes souvenirs made from wood, coral or shells – means that the beautiful places to visit eventually won't be there any more. Over half of the world's coral reefs are at high or medium risk from being totally destroyed, both from visitor-pressure and from being sold as gifts, as well as from climate change. And a survey of more than 240,000 plant species around the world found that one in eight is in danger of extinction. So tread carefully, and don't be seduced by natural souvenirs.

7

SPEAK OUT if you notice any environmental damage caused by the tourism industry in the place you visit

It's not someone else's problem. As a tourist you are directly responsible for the environment in the places you visit. Tell local tour operators about the problem when you are on holiday, and if you booked through an operator in the UK tell them on your return. As a tourist you're responsible for the local environment.

Ethical tourism organisations publish their own codes of conduct for when you are travelling. Familiarise yourself with them and bear them in mind wherever you go. Examples are Friends of Conservation (visit www.foc-uk.com, or call 020 7731 7803), Tourism Concern (visit www.tourismconcern.org.uk, or call 020 7753 3330) and Responsible Travel – visit www.responsibletravel.com.

Tyres

1

In the UK alone, 40 million tyres are scrapped – every year!

Every time you have to change a tyre, consider this: the tyre will probably outlive you by centuries! A tyre will sit in a landfill site for 400 years before it starts to decompose: its components of rubber, oil, sulphur and zinc oxide are designed to last, and in landfill they have no access to the ozone gases that would help break them down. Western Europe generates 200 million scrap tyres each year, 40 million of which come from the UK.

When you take old tyres back to the retailer, make sure their tyre collectors are members of the Responsible Recycler Scheme. Tyre collectors who have signed up to this scheme ensure that wherever possible they recycle old tyres instead of sending them to landfill. 80% of tyres are currently dealt with by these collectors – if your retailer deals with one of the remaining 20% ask them why, and go elsewhere. Details of the scheme can be found at www.tyredisposal.co.uk. You can find out more about tyre recycling from REG Tyre and Automotive Recycling. Visit their website at www.reguk.com or phone them on 01895 444 714.

But there are alternative uses for tyres, too, requiring very little effort.

KIDS – use old tyres to grow potatoes

Put a potato seed in the centre of an old tyre and cover it with 1cm of soil or compost. As the plant grows add soil to just below the growing tip of the shoot, and keep adding more tyres as required. Or if you don't fancy spuds, use an old tyre to make a swing!

— 3 —

Keep tyres pumped up

Under-inflated tyres mean more work for the engine, increasing your fuel consumption by up to 10%. Keep your tyres in good condition by not bumping them against the curb so they last longer and can be re-treaded after use.

Tom got himself re-treaded at the same time as his wheels.

— 4 —

Buy re-treaded tyres

Re-treading only uses half the amount of energy that is needed to replace the whole tyre and has been recognised as the most environmentally-friendly method of dealing with used tyres.

Buy eco-friendly tyres

These avoid the use of non-renewable chemical compounds in the manufacturing process. One example is Goodyear's GT3, which uses a substance derived from maize starch instead of chemical compounds.

_____ 6 _____

Buy products which are made from recycled tyres, such as mouse mats and notebook covers

They look good, work well, and send out the message to everyone who sees them that tyres can be put to all kinds of uses once they've come off the road. Find more from Remarkable Technologies Ltd. Visit www.remarkable.com, or call 020 8741 1234.

_____ 7 _____

Say no to tyre energy plants, such as those used in cement kilns

The high calorific value of tyres means they are often burnt to provide energy. But the damage to the environment caused by these plants far outweighs the benefits of recycling them in this way. The plants give off toxic dioxins (which are recognised carcinogens and affect the immune system and fertility), particulates (which enter the lungs and are too small to be filtered out) and toxic heavy metals. Contact Friends of the Earth for details, at www.foe.co.uk (020 7490 1555).

Go M·A·D!

Volunteering

1

Make a difference to the environment, the community AND yourself!

◆

Nearly half the UK's population – that's 22 million people – already volunteer for something in this country. If you are not one of them, why not? Your time is worth more than your money when it comes to making a difference in the community.

Enjoy cycling, photography, cooking, creative writing? Volunteering enables you to do all those things you've always wanted to do and meet like-minded people. At the same time you will not only be making a positive contribution to the environment, but you will be increasing your employability. Research by Reed Executive found that 70% of employers in 200 top businesses prefer to recruit candidates with volunteering experience on their CV.

There are 400 volunteer bureaux throughout the UK so it's really easy to get involved. Find your nearest bureau at www.navb.org, or call 0121 633 4555. Alternatively, Timebank has a database of volunteering opportunities in the UK and works with 400 TimePartners (local volunteering groups). It matches your skills, interests and the amount of time you can afford to your best-suited voluntary project. Find out more at www.timebank.org.uk, or call 020 7401 5420.

2

KIDS – count creatures!

Join thousands of people aged from 5 to 85 in the UK Phenology Network, that stretches from the Shetlands to the Scilly Isles. They are recording Nature's Calendar - looking for the first signs of autumn and spring by counting the numbers of individuals of different species seen in their local area. All the creatures you count are entered onto an online database that will help build an understanding of climate change and the effect it is having on our woods and wildlife. Contact the Phenology Network at www.phenology.org, or call 01476 581 111.

3

Change places

120,000 schoolchildren and 60,000 adults work on sustainable development projects with Groundwork. These include tree-planting, litter-clearing, graffiti-removal and the changing places initiative (www.changingplaces.org.uk) which transforms derelict land into community gardens or playgrounds. Visit Groundwork's website at www.groundwork.org.uk, or call 0121 236 8565.

4

Join a green gym

Instead of sweating it out alone on the treadmill, a workout session at a Green Gym involves planting hedges, creating wildlife gardens and digging ponds. You can burn almost a third more calories in an hour of footpath building than by doing an aerobics class! Contact the British Trust for Conservation Volunteers (BTCV) for more details. Vvisit www.btcv.org, or call their head office on 01491 821 1600.

Work on a city farm

Feeling city-bound but can't afford long weekend breaks? This is your chance to get into the country without leaving the city. There are sixty city farms across the UK that need your help. Visit www.farmgarden.org.uk, or call 01179 231 800.

— 6 —

Be a community recycler

Volunteer for the Community Recycling Network. Set up by Friends of the Earth, CRN is an umbrella body for about 200 community-based waste projects and businesses. They offer places to 3,000 volunteers and recycling services to 4.5 million people in the UK. As well as doing your bit for recycling, you will be interacting with other volunteers from all over your local community. Phone 0117 942 0142 or visit www.crnhq.demon.co.uk .

— 7 —

Take your good intentions travelling with you – Go MAD abroad

Volunteering doesn't have to be just at home. Ever fancied monitoring turtles, building footbridges in New York State or recreating dry stone walls on Exmoor? A conservation holiday combines travelling to an exciting location, meeting like-minded people and making a difference to the environment at the same time. Surely more of a holiday than lounging on a beach eating ice cream? The British Trust for Conservation Volunteers organises 700 different conservation holidays. Visit www.btcv.org, or call 01491 821 1600 for more details.

Go M·A·D!

Waste

1

We may think of it as waste, but is it?

Each year in the UK we throw away 165 million tonnes of 'waste'. That's the equivalent in weight of 22 million double-decker buses, enough to go around the globe nine times!

Most (80%) of what we automatically describe as waste is recyclable. At present we recycle only 9% in the UK. 90% of our refuse goes to landfills. These emit CO_2 and methane – a greenhouse gas 200 times as powerful as CO_2 – and produce a toxic 'leachate' that seeps into groundwater. Water and oxygen are necessary to break down rubbish but both are in short supply in a landfill, and so the contents take years and years to biodegrade. A newspaper thrown into a landfill is still readable 30 years later.

Landfills impact not only on the environment, but also our pocket. By 2010, the cost of landfill will exceed £55 per tonne – money which could be spent on recycling schemes and waste-reduction initiatives. Rubbish which is not recycled or put in a landfill is incinerated, which is equally harmful, giving off toxic gases into the atmosphere.

There is no such thing as waste in nature – the output from one organism is the input for another. As part of nature we too can take steps to make waste an irrelevant concept.

2
Pick up one piece of litter every day
If every one of us picked up one piece of litter, 60 million pieces of litter would be taken off our streets every day!

3
RECYCLE!
The Zero Waste strategy in New Zealand has proved that by minimising waste in the first place and maximising recycling, incineration is unnecessary and the amount of rubbish going to landfill can be cut by 90%. (See www.zerowaste.co.nz, and the website of Defenders of the Ouse Valley and Estuary, which is setting up policy groups for a Zero Waste strategy in the UK, at www.dove2000.org). You may conscientiously recycle your bottles and paper but how about oil, stamps, spectacles, office equipment, mobile phones and rubble? You can locate your nearest recycling point by going to www.wastepoint.co.uk/wasteconnect or www.recycle-more.com. Enter your postcode and the type of waste you want to recycle.

4
RE-USE!
If each of the UK's 10 million office workers used one less staple a day by re-using a paper clip, that could save 120 tonnes of steel each year. Even the tiniest things can still be used wastefully. Only use a new product if there is no re-usable alternative.

REDUCE!

90% of the material used in the production of, or contained within consumer goods, becomes waste within six weeks of sale. Reduce the amount of disposable products you buy and always look for alternatives which will last.

6

RESEARCH

Find out about your local council's recycling schemes and campaign for them to be improved by writing to them and to your local MP. As well as its environmental benefits, recycling creates jobs. For every million tonnes of waste processed, landfill creates 40–60 jobs, incineration creates 100–290 jobs, and recycling 400–590 jobs.

7

REACT! – Say NO! to incineration

Dioxins, furans, acid gases, heavy metals... these are just some of the toxic pollutants created by incineration plants. Among the risks these can pose to health are hormonal defects, reduced immune system capacity, and lung and kidney disease. But the UK government plans to press ahead with the creation of 130 new waste incinerators, each one burning up to 250,000 tonnes of rubbish a year.

This is propagating the waste problem rather than tackling it from the roots – the millions spent on incineration plants should, and could, be spent on waste reduction and recycling initiatives instead. Visit Friends of the Earth at www.foe.co.uk/campaigns/waste/issues/incineration, or call 020 7490 1555.

Go M·A·D!

Water

1

Water is our most valuable resource

It rains so much in the UK that water, you might imagine, should never be in short supply. Yet we use water today in so many ways that the average person in the UK now washes away a staggering 1,050 litres of water a week.

The result of our heavy usage is a lowering of the natural water table, and although we are capable of building more and more reservoirs to look after our needs, these disrupt both natural hydrological systems and local wildlife. In addition, transporting water from reservoirs to meet local needs uses vast amounts of energy, as well as adding to the complex infrastructure of piping that crosses our land.

Much of the water we use, too, has undergone quite a transformation since it first fell from the sky. Used water is treated with chemicals, which find their way back into the environment when we use it a second time. Even ultra-violet light is now part of the used water treatment process.

And yet water is a natural resource that we can conserve with very little effort.

2

Use short bursts of water from the tap when your brushing your teeth

Just using it in spurts to rinse your toothbrush can save 80% of the water that you normally use.

3

Put a brick in your toilet cistern

A third of an average family's water use is flushed down the toilet. Every flush uses 12 litres of water – with a brick or a water-filled plastic tub in your toilet cistern you will save over 3,000 litres a year.

4

Kit out your house with water-saving devices

Spray taps let out a smaller volume of water but achieve the same results as normal taps. Low-flow showerheads can be fitted to maximise water coverage and minimise the water used. And a dual-flush toilet saves thousands of litres a year by discharging a small amount of water for liquid waste and a larger amount for solid waste. Contact the Centre for Alternative Energy for more details at www.cat.org, or call 01654 702 400.

Only use a washing machine when you have a full load

A single washing machine cycle uses up to 100 litres of water, and the average family uses their washing machine five times a week. That's 26,000 litres a year.

Why use drinking water for flushing the toilet, washing your clothes and watering your plants? Use rainwater!

Flushing the loo accounts for over a third of our water use, laundry for 12% and irrigation for 7%. To really make a difference, invest in a rainwater collection system that will enable you to use rainwater for all these activities. But if that's a bit daunting, install a large water butt for your gardening and some washing needs. Contact the Centre for Alternative Technology for advice www.cat.org.uk (01654 702 400)

Help bring clean water to the billion people who need it

We take water for granted. But over a billion people in the world don't have safe water to drink. That's one in six of the world's population. And 2.4 billion don't have access to adequate sanitation. Water Aid and Tearfund's campaign 'Water Matters' is petitioning the UK government to put water and sanitation high on the agenda at the Earth Summit 2002. Find out all about the campaign at www.watermatters.org.uk or contact WaterAid to keep informed about the global water crisis at www.wateraid.org.uk (020 7793 4500). And meanwhile make sure your own water authority isn't wasting your water bills: in some areas of the UK more than a third of water is lost through leaking pipes. Find out from OFWAT (www.ofwat.gov.uk, or call 0121 625 1373) what your authority's record is and if it's bad, write to them to protest that consumers should not have to pay rising costs if the company won't invest more of its profits in water conservation.

Wood

1

The planet needs trees to help it breathe

◆

The average person in the UK consumes the equivalent of 5 tea-chests of wood each year, that's 30 times as much used by the average person in India. In the tropics 17 million hectares of forest are destroyed each year, causing the extinction of 75 animal species a day. But the problem is not confined to the tropics: in developed countries, natural forests are being replaced by faster-growing 'factory forests' for paper production, endangering thousands of species. International companies have now begun to clear-fell vast tracts of previously untouched forests in the former Soviet Union.

It's not only biodiversity that's at risk. Old-growth forests are massive storehouses of carbon that is released into the atmosphere when they are destroyed. Deforestation in the tropics accounts for 22% of global CO_2 emissions. The United Nations has predicted a 58% increase in wood consumption over the next 20 years. So every saving you make on your use of wood will help the world breathe just that little bit easier.

'...lovely holiday, terrific souvenirs but not a tree to get any shade under!...'

2

Look for the Forest
Stewardship Council symbol

When you buy wood with the FSC label you know it comes from a
sustainable source managed to strict environmental, social and
economic standards. In 1997, the Brazilian Government admitted 80%
of the timber extracted from the rainforest was obtained illegally,
often involving the invasion of indigenous lands. A World Bank report
found that 80% of Indonesian timber products are also illegal. So
certification is vital. And 'wooden' products don't just include the
obvious ones: make sure the charcoal you buy is also FSC accredited.
We burn 60,000 tonnes of charcoal each year in the UK, 95% of which
is imported and often comes from endangered woodland habitat.
Visit www.fsc-uk.demon.co.uk, or call 01686 413 916.

3

When you buy wooden carvings, at
home or abroad, make sure they come
from a sustainable source

Each year, 50,000 hardwood trees are used to carve holiday souvenirs
or gifts in UK shops. Fifty species of tree are exploited by this
$20 million industry. Kenyan woodcarvings are a tempting present –
but only buy them if they are guaranteed to come from a fast-growing
forest. Neem is an excellent alternative to endangered hardwood.

4

Buy reclaimed wood

Thousands of tonnes of wood are thrown away by the wood trade
each year. But increasingly companies, are 'reclaiming' this waste
wood so it can be used again. Get a copy of the Good Wood Guide
from Friends of the Earth, which has advice on where to get hold of
second-hand wooden furniture and products made from reclaimed
wood. Visit www.foe.co.uk, or call 020 7490 1555.

— 5 —

Bring trees back into your local area

One hectare of woodland grown to maturity will absorb the carbon emissions of 100 average family cars driven for one year, and a large beech tree can provide enough oxygen for the daily requirement of ten people. Organise a community tree planting project, or dedicate a tree to a friend as a present. Contact Trees for London (www.treesforlondon.org.uk or call 020 7587 1320) or the Woodland Trust (www.woodland-trust.org.uk or call 01476 581 135) for more details.

— 6 —

Only use boron-based wood preservatives

Wood preservatives are designed to kill. Designed to kill pests, maybe, but the pesticides they contain are nerve poisons and their fungicides are toxins that harm the environment during production and continue to do so after they have been used. Look on the packet to make sure that the preservatives you use are made from boron, which is far less harmful and is the only kind approved of by the Association for Environment Conscious Building (www.aecb.net or 01559 370 908). AURO is a company specialising in environmental finishes. Visit www.auroorganic.co.uk, or call 01799 543 077.

— 7 —

Protect your local forest

We only have 2% of our ancient woodland left and it's fast disappearing. Broadleaf woodland is home to 50% of the UK's threatened species – more than any other habitat in the UK – and they are irreplaceable, so it's essential that we stop their destruction. Get a copy of the Woodland Trust's free guide 'Is your local wood under threat?' to find out what steps you can take to help save it. Contact the Woodland Trust on 01476 581 135 or at www.woodland-trust.org.uk. Also, write to the Swedish and Finnish governments to ask them to stop replacing ancient snow forests with factory forests. Snow forests are home to a variety of species, such as brown bears, lynx, wolves and woodpeckers. Friends of the Earth has sample letters at www.foe.co.uk or ring them on 020 7490 1555.

Working

1

Business and ecology have more in common than you might think

'Ecology' and 'Economics' are both derived from the Greek word Oikos, meaning home or household – but language aside, both involve resource availability, supply and demand, competition, and costs.

In the natural world, these costs are paid in energy and resources while in the world of work they are paid in money – a business cannot grow without capital just as an ecosystem cannot support itself and us when its resources are depleted. But increasingly businesses are realising the role that they play in ecosystems, both due to their own use of resources and the increasing pressure from customers to clean up their act and become more sustainable.

However, a recent survey revealed that 45% of directors and chief executives of major businesses across the UK had not even heard of sustainable development, so there's a lot of work to be done! A good way to describe sustainability is the ability of the present generation to meet its own needs whilst not compromising the ability of future generations to meet their own.

Sound over-ambitious? Not if you take it step by step.

Put a spider plant on your desk

Indoor plants are a natural air conditioner and can remove up to 87% of indoor pollution in 24 hours.

— 3 —

Use mugs or glasses not disposable cups in the office

In the UK, 5 billion disposable plastic cups are thrown away each year. If your company is guilty, get in contact with Remarkable Pencils, which produces 20,000 pens and pencils a day from recycled plastic cups. Visit www.remarkable.co.uk, or call 020 8741 1234. And buy coffee, milk and sugar in bulk.

'They won't last long in this job, they'll be here today, gone tomorrow'

— 4 —

Save paper! Put technology to work and keep a box for recycling

Each year the average person in the UK uses 20,000 sheets of A4 at work, and over 350 million trees are cut down for office paper. For every person in an office an average of 39kg of waste paper each month is NOT recycled – for a department of 10 people this amounts to 40 sacks of paper going to landfill sites. Avoid printing hard copy from the electronic system whenever possible. Choose photocopiers, printers and fax machines that can cope with all types of recycled paper and can produce double-sided copies. And make sure you close the loop – buy recycled stationery as well. Find out more from the Green Stationery Company, visit www.greenstat.co.uk, or call 01223 480556; or visit Recycled Paper Supplies at www.recycled-paper.co.uk.

Ask your business to send an energy management email to every employee

When Rover sent an energy management newsletter to its employees at its Longbridge car plant, with simple energy saving tips, total energy savings worth £1 million were achieved in just six months.

Recycle or re-fill your ink cartridges

Over six million toner cartridges are used in the UK every year and consumption is rising by 15% per year. It is estimated that half of these end up in landfill sites. Phone the Recycling Helpline 0800 435576 for details of recycling schemes, many of which are organised by charities. Or refill your own. Find out how at www.refilltoner.com.

Transform your company

Get expert advice on how to make your company more sustainable and environmentally friendly: Contact Business in the Environment at www.business-in-environment.org.uk (0870 600 2482), or The National Centre for Business and Sustainability at www.thencbs.co.uk (0161 295 5276). Make sure the advice reaches all the right people and is acted on! Friends of the Earth also publishes a Green Office Action Plan. Get your copy from www.foe-scotland.org.uk/pubs/pubs_index.html. Also, encourage your company to publish its environmental and social accounts. This involves taking a detailed audit not only of its financial progress but also of its effect on the environment and society, hence making the company accountable to its stakeholders. Companies which have already done this included Camelot, The Body Shop, Traidcraft, the Co-operative Wholesale Society and Ben and Jerry's. To find out more go to the New Economics Foundation www.neweconomics.org or go straight to the Institute for Social and Ethical Accountability at www.accountability.org.uk.

Go M·A·D!

Contacts

How do I find out more?

Make that telephone call, write that letter! Here is an alphabetical list of all the organisations referred to in Go MAD! But first – get in touch with us!

Go MAD is all about interaction, so please let us know of any organisations or initiatives you feel should be mentioned in the book, as well any new environmental tips. You can send your idea by post or email and if we use it we'll send you a free copy of next year's edition of Go MAD! Send your idea to:

Email: watchdog@thinkpublishing.co.uk
Post: Go MAD! tips, The Ecologist, Unit 18,
Chelsea Wharf, 15 Lots Road, London, SW10 0QJ

Remember to include your name, address and contact phone number to ensure you receive the next edition of Go MAD!

Adbusters [p132]
www.adbusters.org

Amnesty International
99 Roseberry Avenue, London EC1R
4RE
(020) 7814 6200

**Association for Environment
Conscious Building [p44]**
PO Box 32, Llandysul SA44 5ZA
(01559) 370 908

**AURO Organic Paint
Supplies Ltd [p163]**
Unit 2 Pamphillions Farm, Debden,
Saffron Waldon CB11 3JD
(01799) 543 077

Baby Milk Action [p13]
23 St Andrew's Street,
Cambridge CB2 3AX
(01223) 464 420

Babynat Organico [p13]
60-62 King's Road, Reading RG1 3AA
(0118) 951 0518

Barn Owl Trust [p124]
Waterleat, Ashburton,
Devon TQ13 7HU
(01364) 653 026

Bats Conservation Trust [p66]
15 Cloisters House, 8 Battersea Park
Road, London SW8 4BG
(020) 7627 2629

167

Battersea Dogs' Home [p117]
4 Battersea Park Road,
London SW8 4AA
(020) 7622 3626

Beauty Without Cruelty [p37]
74 Oldfield Rd, Hampton, TW12 2HR
(020) 8979 8156

Best Foot Forward
The Future Centre, 115 Magdalen
Road, Oxford OX4 1RQ
(01865) 250 818

Bicycle Beano [p39]
Erwood, Builtwells, LD2 3PQ
(01982) 560 471

**BioRegional
Development Group [p28]**
Sutton Ecology Centre, Honeywood
Walk, Carshalton SM5 3NX
(020) 8773 2322

Bluepet [p115]
Unit 2, 14 The Green, Hartshill,
Nuneaton, Warwickshire, CV10 0SW
(02476) 396 961

**The Body Shop
International Plc [p34]**
Watersnead, Little Hampton, West
Sussex, BN17 6LS
Head Office: (01903) 731 500

BORN [p12]
64 Gloucester Road, Bishopston,
Bristol, BS7 8BH
(0117) 924 5080

**British Association of Fair Trade
Shops [p145]**
c/o Gateway World Shop, Market
Place, Durham, DH1 3NJ
(0118) 9569361

**British Astronomical Association
(Campaign for Dark Skies) [p94]**
Burlington House, Piccadilly, London,
W1J 0DU
(020) 7734 4145

**British Complementary Medicine
Association [p76]**
174 Manor Lane, London SE1 8LP
(01242) 519911

**Glass Manufacturers
Confederation [p70]**
Northumberland Road,
Sheffield S10 2UA
(0114) 268 6201

**British Trust for Conservation
Workers [p153/154]**
36 St Mary's Street, Wallingford, Oxon
OX10 0EU
(01491) 839 766

British Union Against Vivisection [p37]
16A Crane Grove, London N7 8NN
(020) 7700 4888

British Waterways [p142]
Willow Grange, Church Road,
Watford, WD17 4QA
(01923) 226 422

Business in the Environment [p166]
137 Shepherdess Walk,
London N1 7RQ
(0870) 600 2482

Butterfly Conservation [p73]
Manor Yard, East Dulworth, Wareham,
Dorset BH20 5QP
(01929) 400 209

The Campaign for Real Food [p99]
107 Blackshaw Road, London, SW17
0BU
(020) 7771 0099

**Care, Rehabilitation and Aid for Sick
Hedgehogs (C.R.A.S.H.) [p72]**
45 Culliford Crescent, Canford Heath,
Poole, Dorset BH17 9ET
(01202) 699 358

**Centre for Alternative Energy
[p48/58/59/79160]**
Machynlleth, Powys SY20 9AZ
(01654) 702 400

The Charity Commission [p19]
2nd floor, 20 Kings Parade, Queens
Dock, Liverpool L3 4DQ
(0870) 333 0123

Community Car Share Network [p16]
The Studio, 32 The Calls,
Leeds LS2 7EW
(01132) 349 299

Community Composting Network [p31]
67 Alexandra Road, Sheffield S2 3EE
(0114) 258 0483

Compassion in World Farming [p61]
Charles House, 5A Charles St,
Petersfield, Hampshire, G32 3EH
(01730) 264 208

Computer Aid International [p139]
114 Belgravia Workshops, 159
Malborough Road, London N19 4NF
(020) 7281 0091

Community Computers [p139]
(0113) 293 0168
www.community-computers.co.uk

Computers for Charity [p139]
PO Box 48, Bude, Cornwall EX23 8BL
(01288) 361 199

**Community Recycling
Network [p154]**
Trelawney House, Surrey Street,
Bristol BS2 8PS
(0117) 942 0142

Community Repaint [p45]
c/o SWAP, 74 Kirkgate,
Leeds LS2 7DJ
(0113) 243 8777

Co-operative Bank [p87]
PO Box 101, 1 Balloon Street,
Manchester, M60 4EP
(0161) 832 3456

Corporate Watch [p133]
16B Cherwell Street,
Oxford, OX4 1BG
(01865) 791 391

**Countryside Foundation for
Education [p55]**
PO Box 8, Hebden Bridge, West
Yorkshire HX7 5YJ
(01422) 885 566

Critical Mass [p38]
www.critical-mass.org

Culpeper Herbalists [p36]
Hadstock Road, Linton,
Cambridge, CB1 6NJ
(01223) 891 196

Cyclist's Touring Club HQ [p40]
Cotterell House, 69 Meadrow,
Godalming, Surrey GU7 3HS
(01483) 417 217

**The Day Chocolate
Company [p19]**
4 Gainsford Street,
London, SE1 2NE
(020) 7378 6550

The Deodorant Stone (UK) Ltd [p85]
2 Lime Tree Cottage, Foxley,
Malmesbury, Wiltshire SN16 0JJ
(01666) 826 515

Directory Recycling Project [p112]
c/o Are You Doing Your Bit?
DEFRA, Zone 6/F5, Ashdown House,
123 Victoria Street,
London SW1E 6DE
0800 783 1592

**Dove (The Defenders of the Ouse
Valley and Estuary) [p156]**
www.dove2000.org

Earthscan [p127]
120 Pentonville Road, London N1 9JN
(020) 7278 0433

Earthwise Baby [p102]
Aspley Distribution Ltd, PO Box 1708,
Aspley Guise, Milton Keynes MK17
8YA
(01908) 587 275

Eco-Babes [p102]
79 Orton Drive, Witchford, Ely,
Cambridgeshire CB6 2JG
(01353) 664 941

Ecozone [p21/22]
Unit 1 Tannery Close, Beckenham,
Kent BR3 4BY
(0870) 600 6969

Ecology Building Society [p88]
18 Station Road, Crosshills, Keighley,
BD2 7EH
(0845) 674 5566

Ecover UK Ltd [p109]
165 Main Street, New Greenham Park,
Thatcham, West Berkshire RG19 6HN
(01635) 528 240

**Eco Solutions Ltd
(and Strip Paint) [p45]**
Summerleaze House, Church Road,
Winscombe BS25 1BH
(01934) 844 484

ECOS Organic Paints [p45]
Unit 34 Heysham Business Park,
Middleton Road, Heysham, LA3 3PP
(01524) 852 371

Electric Car Association [p16]
Blue Lias House, Station Road, Hatch
Beauchamp TA3 6SQ
(01823) 480 196

The Empty Homes Agency [p45]
195-197 Victoria Street, London SW1E
5NE
(020) 7828 6288

Energy Efficiency [p56]
c/o BRECSU, BRE Ltd, Garston,
Watford WD2 7JR
0800 585 794

**Energy+, Environmental Change
Institute [p91]**
5 South Parks Road, Oxford OX1 3UB
(01865) 281 123

Energy Saving Trust [p56]
21 Dartmouth Street, London SW1H
9BP
(0845) 727 7200

Energy Saving Installers [p79]
21 Dartmouth Street, London SW1H
9BP
(0845) 727 7200

Energy Star [p139]
www.energystar.gov

The Environment Agency [p130]
Phone 0800 9333 111 to locate your
nearest EA office.

**The Environmental Investigation
Agency (EIA) [p139]**
62-63 Upper Street, London N1 0NY
(020) 7354 7960

Environmental Mobile Control [p139]
Unit 3 Glensyl Way, Hawkins Lane
Industrial Estate, Burton on Trent,

Staffordshire DE14 1LX
(01283) 516 259

**Environmental Transport Association
[p16/88]**
10 Church Street, Weybridge KT13
8RS
(01932) 828 882

Ethical Consumer [p23/131/133]
Unit 21, 41 Old Birley Street,
Manchester M15 5RF
(0161) 226 2929

**Ethical Investment Research Service
(EIRIS) [p88]**
80-84 Bondway, London SW8 1SF
(020) 7840 5700

Ethical Junction [p131/124]
1st floor, Dale House, 35 Dale Street,
Manchester M1 2HF
(0161) 236 3637

Ethical Matters [p131]
Unit A2, 2nd floor, Linton House, 39-
51 Highgate Road, London, NW5 1RS
(020) 7419 7258

Ethical Will [p43]
www.ethicalwill.com

Fairtrade Foundation [p48/58]
Suite 204, 16 Baldwins Gardens,
London EC1N 7RJ
(020) 7405 5942

Farm Around, Offices [p106]
B140-143, New Covent Garden, Nine
Elms Lane, London SW8 5PA
(020) 7627 8066

**Federation of City Farms and
Community Gardens [p142]**
The Green House, Hereford Street,
Bedminster, Bristol BS3 4NA
(0117) 923 1800

Festival Eye [p97]
BCM 2002, London WC1 N 3XX
(0870) 737 1011

Forest Stewardship Council [p45/162]
Unit D Station Building, Llanidloes,
Powys, SY18 6EB
(01686) 413 916

Freewheelers [p16]
www.freewheelers.com

The Fresh Food Company [p106]
326 Portobello Road,
London W10 5RU
(020) 8969 0351

The Fresh Water Filter [p130]
895 High Road, Essex RN6 4HL
(020) 8597 3223

Friends of Conservation [p148]
Riverbank House,
1 Putney Bridge Approach,
London SW6 3JD
(020) 7731 7803

**Friends of the Earth
[p58/96/157/151/162]**
26-28 Underwood Street,
London N1 7JQ
(020) 7490 1555

**The Funeral Company
Limited [p43]**
19 Stratford Road, Milton Keynes
MK12 5LJ
(01908) 225 222

Gossypium [p12/106]
2-3 St Andrew's Place,
Southover Road, Lewes,
East Sussex BN7 1UP
(01273) 897 509

Green Books [p127]
Foxhole, Dartington, Totnes TQ9 6EB
(01803) 863 260

Green Building Store [p44]
11 Huddersfield Road, Meltham,
Holmsirth, HD9 4NJ
(01484) 854 898

Green Globe Accreditations [p82]
45 High Street, Royal Tonbridge
Wells, Kent TN1 1XL
(01892) 541 717

The Green Guide [p131]
271 Upper Street, London N1 2UQ
(020) 7354 2709

Green Prices [p58]
www.greenprices.com

The Green Shop [p21]
Cheltenham Road, Bisley,
Gloucestershire GL6 7BX
(01452) 770 629

**The Green Stationery
Company [p99/112]**
Studio 1, 114 Walcot Street,
Bath BA1 5BG
(01225) 480 556

Greenpeace [p22/58]
Canonbury Villas,
London N1 2PN
(020) 7865 8100

Greyhound Rescue [p142]
(020) 7188 1068
www.greyhoundrescue.co.uk

Groundwork [p28]
85-87 Cornwall Street,
Birmingham B3 3BY
(0121) 236 8565

**The Guide to
Aromatherapy [p36]**
www.fragrant.demon.co.uk/ukaromas.
html

The Hawk and Owl Trust [p124]
c/o the Zoological Society
of London, Regents Park,
London NW1 4RY
(01582) 832 182

The Healthy House [p106]
Cold Harbour, Ruscombe, Stroud,
Gloucestershire GL6 6DA
(01453) 752 216

The Hemp Shop [p112]
22 Gardner Street, North Laine,
Brighton BN1 1UP
(07041) 31 32 33

The Hemp Union [p112]
24 Anlaby Road, Hull, East
Yorks HU1 2PA
(01482) 225 328

**Henry Doubleday Research
Association [p30/65]**
Ryton Organic Gardens, Coventry,
CV8 3LG
(0247) 6 303 517

Hipp Organic [p13]
Hipp GMBH & Co, Vertribe KG,
Georg Hipp Strasse, 85276
Psassenhofen, Germany
(0845) 050 1351

**The Improvement and Development
Agency (IDEA) (for LA21) [p28]**
Layden House, 76-78 Turnmill Street,
London EC1M 5LG
(020) 7296 6599

**Institute of Social and Ethnic
Accountability [p166]**
Unit A, 137 Shepherdess Walk,
London, N1 7RQ
(020) 7549 0400

**International Dark Sky
Association [p94]**
3225 N. First Avenue, Tuscon,
Arizona, 85719 USA
(520) 293 3198

Juice [p58]
0800 316 2610
www.npower.com/juice
See npower or Greenpeace

Juniper Green [p105]
Meadow View House, Tannery Lane,
Bramley, Surrey GU5 0AB
(01483) 894 650

**La Leche League (breastfeeding
support) [p12]**
BM Box 3424, London WC1N 3XX
(020) 7242 1278

Lightswitch [p94]
Rose House, 109A South End,
Croydon CR0 1BG
(08705) 133 538

**Local Exchange Trading System
(LETS) [p28/46/57]**
12 Southcote Road, London N19 5BJ
(Send six loose stamps if you want to
receive the information booklet).
020 7607 7852

LP Gas Association [p16]
Pavilion 16, Headlands Business Park,
Salisbury Road, Ringwood, Hampshire
BH24 3PE
(01425) 461612

**The Mailing Preference Service
[p111]**
Freepost 22, London W1E 7EZ
(020) 7766 4410

Mast Action UK [p139]
MAUK Head Office, P.O. Box 312,
Hertfordshire EN7 5ZE
www.mastaction.org

More Food for Thought [p100]
31 Neal Street, Covent Garden,
London, WC2H 9PR
(020) 7836 9072

The Nappy Lady [p103]
16 Hill Brow, Bearsted, Maidstone,
Kent ME14 4AW
(01622) 739 034

**The National Association
of Farmers' Markets [p60/133]**
South Vaults, Green Park Station,
Bath BA1 1JB
(send a large SAE)
(01225) 787 914

**The National Association
of Nappy Washing Services [p103]**
Call (0121) 693 4949 to find
out your nearest NWS.

**The National Association of
Volunteer Bureau [p152]**
New Oxford House, 16 Waterloo
Street, Birmingham B2 5UG
(0121) 633 4555

**The National Canine
Defence League [p116]**
17 Wakley Street,
London EC1V 7RQ
(020) 7837 0006

**The National Centre for Business
and Sustainability [p166]**
Peel Buildings,
University of Salford,
Manchester M5 4WT
(0161) 295 5276

National Childbirth Trust [p12]
Alexandra House, Oldham Terrace,
Acton, London W3 6NH
(020) 8992 2616
Breastfeeding line: (0870) 444 708

National Energy Foundation [p79]
The National Centre,
Dady Avenue, Knowhill,
Milton Keynes MK5 8NG
(01908) 665 555
Free advice line: 0800 512 012

National Recycling Forum [p132]
c/o Wastewatch, 96 Tooley Street,
London SE1 2TH
(020) 7089 2100

**The National Society of Allotment
and Leisure Gardens [p67]**
O'Dell House, Hunters Road,
Corby, Northants NN17 5JE
(01536) 266 576

Natural Death Centre [p43]
20 Heber Road,
London NW2 6AA
(020) 8208 2853

Natural Friends [p96]
15 Benyon Gardens, Culford, Bury St
Edmunds, Suffolk IP28 6EA
(01284) 728 315

New Economics Foundation [p166]
Cinnamon House, 6-8 Cole Street,
London SE1 4YH
(020) 7089 2800

NHS Organ Donor Net [p43]
UK Transplant, Fox Den Road,
Stoke Gifford, Bristol, BS34 8RR.
Organ donor information line:
(0845) 60 60 400

**Norwich and Peterborough Building
Society [p87]**
Principle Office, Peterborough
Business Park Lynchwood,
Peterborough, PE2 6W2
(0845) 300 6727

Npower [p56]
Dorcan House, Eldene Drive,
Swindon, Wiltshire SN3 3SH
0800 389 2388

**Offices of Water Services (OFWAT)
[p160]**
Centre City Tower, 7 Hill Street,
Birmingham, B5 4UA
(0121) 625 1373

Oil Bank [p15]
c/o the Environment Agency,
Rivers House, Waterside Drive,
Aztec West, Almondsbury,
Bristol BS12 4UD
0800 66 33 66

**Organic Consumers' Association
[p61]**
6101 Cliff Estate Road,
Little Marais, MN 55614
United States
(00 218) 226 4164

Organic Delivery Company [p106]
70 Rivington Street,
London EC2A 3AY
(020) 7739 8181

Organic Wine Company [p105]
PO Box 81, High Wycombe,
Bucks HP13 5QN
(01494) 446 557

Oxfam [p24]
Head Office, 247 Banbury Road,
Oxford, 0X2 7D2
(01865) 311 311

**Pesticide Action
Network UK [p113]**
Eurolink Centre Unit 16,
49 Effra Road, London SW2 1BZ
(020) 7274 8895

The Phenology Network [p153]
Alton Park, Dyfart Way, Grantham
NG31 6LL
(01476) 581 111

The Phone Co-op [p87]
5 The Mill House, Elmsfield
Business Centre, Worscester Road,
Chipping Norton OX7 5XL
(0845) 458 9000

Plantlife [p31]
21 Elizabeth Street,
London SW1W 9RP
(020) 7808 0100

Powabyke Ltd [p40]
Unit 6, Riverside Business Park,
Lower Bristol Road,
Bath BA2 3DW
(01225) 787 177

Powerplus [p16]
42 St Leonards Road, Eastbourne,
East Sussex, BN21 3UU
(01323) 417 700

Pure H2O [p130]
Unit 5, Egham Business Village,
Crabtree Road, Egham,
Surrey TW20 8RB
(01784) 221 188

The Real Nappy Association [p103]
Sustainable Wales, 1st Floor, 41 John
Street, Porthcawl CF36 3AP
(01656) 783 405

Reclaim the Streets [p97]
62 Fieldgate Street, London E1 1ES
(020) 7281 4621

Re-Cycle [p39]
60 High Street, West Mersea,
Essex CO5 8JE
(01206) 382 207

Recycle More [p110/156]
c/o Valpak Ltd, Savannah House,
11-12 Charles II Street,
London SW1Y 4QJ
(020) 7321 3500

Recycled Paper Supplies [p112]
Gate Farm, Fen End, Kenilworth, CV8
1NW
(01676) 533 832

Recycling Helpline [p99]
0800 435576 (will put you through to
you local council's recycling
department)

Refill Toner Ltd [p166]
305 Telsen Centre, Thomas Street,
Aston, Birmingham B6 4TN
(0121) 693 2644

REG-UK [p149]
191 High Street, Yiewsley, West
Drayton, Middlesex UB7 7XW
(01895) 444714

**Remarkable Technologies Inc
[p151/165]**
Inc. 56 Glentham Road,
London SW13 9JJ
(020) 8741 1234

Responsible Travel [p148]
www.responsibletravel.com

RSPCA [p116/117]
Wilberforce Way, Southwater,
Horsham, West Sussex RH13 9RS
(0870) 333 5999

Save Waste and Prosper [p45]
74 Kirkgate, Leeds LS2 7DJ
(0113) 243 8777

**Sawdays Special
Places to Stay [p81]**
The Home Farm Stables,
Barrow Court Lane,
Barrow Gurney,
Bristol BS48 3RW
(01275) 464891

Scope [p24]
PO Box 833 Milton Keynes MK12 5NY
(0808) 800 3333

School Energy [p55]
Kenley House, 25 Bridgeman Terrace,
Wigan, WN1 1TD
(0870) 7000 457 or (01942) 332 273

**Schools Waste Action Club (SWAC)
[p54]**
c/o Waste Watch, Ground Floor,
Europa House, 13-17 Ironmonger
Row, London, EC1V 3QG
(0870 243 0136)

Simply Soaps [p13/84]
Brillig, Rackheath Path,
Norwich NR13 6LP
(07775) 564 802

The Slow Food Movement [p34]
via Mendicita Istruita 14,
12042 Bra CN, Italy
0800 917 1232

Soil Association [p51/104-106]
Bristol House, Victoria Street,
Bristol BS1 6BY
(0117) 929 0661

SolaLighting Ltd [p93]
1 Newton Road, Wollaston,
Wellingborough,
Northamptonshire NN29 7QN
(0845) 458 0101

Spirit of Nature Ltd [p85]
Units 1 & 2 Clipstone Brook Industrial
Park, Cherrycourt Way, Leighton
Buzzard, Bedfordshire LU7 4GP
(0870) 725 9885

Surfers Against Sewage [p88]
Wheal Kitty Workshops, St Agnes,
Cornwall TR5 0RD
(01872) 553 001

**Sustain: The Alliance for Better
Food and Farming [p104/106]**
94 White Lion Street,
London N1 9PF
(Send an A4 s.a.e)
(020) 7837 1228

**Sustrans (Safe Routes to Schools
Information Team) [p54]**
c/o 35 King Street, Bristol BS1 4DZ
(0117) 9268893

Textile Recycling Association [p24]
16 High Street, Brampton,
Huntingdon,
Cambridgeshire PE28 4TU
(01480) 455 249

Timebank [p19/152]
The Mezzanine, Elizabeth House,
39 York Road, London SE1 7NQ
(020) 7401 5420

**The Totnes Genetics Group (TOGG)
[p61]**
PO Box 77, Totnes TQ9 5ZJ
(01803) 840098

Tourism Concern [p148]
Stapleton House, 277-281 Holloway
Road, London N7 8HN
(020) 7753 3330

Toxic Kitchen [p22]
c/o Greenpeace, Canonbury Villas,
London N1 2PN
(01179) 268 893

Tradewatch [p135]
www.citizen.org

Traffic International [p118]
219C Huntingdon Road,
Cambridge CB3 0DL
(01223) 277 427

Traidcraft Plc [p145]
Kingsway, Gateshead, Tyne and Wear
NE11 0NE
(0191) 491 0591

Trees for London [p163]
Prince Consort Lodge,
Kennington Park,
Kennington Park Place,
London SE11 4AS
(020) 7587 1320

Triodos Bank [p87]
Freepost BS9292,
Bristol BS8 3BR
(01179) 739 339

Unit-E [p58]
Freepost SCE9229, Chippenham
SN15 1UZ
(0845) 601 1410

Used Tyre Working Group [p149]
www.tyredisposal.co.uk

uSwitch [p58]
Customer Services,
Victoria Station House,
191 Victoria Street
London SW1E 5NE
(0845) 601 2856

Vision Aid Overseas [p70]
12 The Bell Centre, Newton Road,
Crawley, West Sussex RH10 9F2
(01259) 353 5016

Wasteconnect [p91/120/156]
Old Stables, Glansevern Hall, Berriew,
Welshpool, Powys SY21 8AH
(01686) 640 600

Waste Watch Wasteline [p30/54]
96 Tooley Street, London SE1 2TH
(0870) 243 0136

Water Matters [p160]
Prince Consort House, 27-29 Albert
Embankment, London SE1 7UB
(020) 7793 4500

Wiggly Wigglers [p30]
Lower Blakemere Farm, Blakemere,
Herefordshire HR2 9PX
(01981) 500 391
Helpline: 0800 216 990

**The Wildfowl and
Wetlands Trust [p142]**
Slimbridge, Gloucestershire GL2 7BT
(01453) 891 900

**Wildlife Trusts – UK Operations
Centre [p124]**
The Kiln, Waterside, Mather Road,
Newark, Nottinghamshire NG24 1WT
(01636) 677 711

**Women's Environmental
Network [p103]**
PO Box 30626, London E1 1TZ
(020) 7481 9004

Woodcraft Folk [p27]
13 Ritherdon Road,
London SW17 8QE
(020) 8672 6031

The Woodland Trust [p162]
Autumn Park, Grantham,
Lincolnshire NG31 6LL.
National Enquiry line:
(01476) 581 135

**World Development
Movement [p55]**
25 Beehive Place,
London SW9 7QR
(020) 7737 6215

WWF-UK [p51]
Panda House,
Weyside Park, Godalming,
Surrey GU7 1XR
(01483) 426 444

Zerowaste [p156]
www.zerowaste.co.nz

The funny drawings in Go MAD! have been concocted by cartoonist STAN EALES

Email: stan@staneales.freeserve.co.uk
Phone & Fax: 44 0208 682 1894
Web: www.staneales.freeserve.co.uk

Magazines
Punch • Private Eye • The Spectator • The Ecologist

Greetings Cards
Hallmark • Camden Graphics • Hanson White • Paper house

Books
'Isn't Progress Wonderful?' • 'Cashtoons'

STEWARDSHIP ETHICAL FUNDS

THE **WORLD'S** A **BETTER PLACE** WITH **FRIENDS**

Investing in a Friends Provident Stewardship Ethical Fund can really make a world of difference – both to you and your family's long term future and the planet we all live on.

That's because we only invest in companies which provide excellent long term growth potential, but also make a positive contribution to society and the environment.

The Friends Provident Stewardship Fund was the UK's first ethical investment and today, standing at over £1.3 billion in size, it remains the market leader.* To find out more, call **0800 00 00 80** today.

FRIENDS PROVIDENT